THE
AMISH
of Illinois' Heartland

THE
AMISH
of Illinois' Heartland

For Jane – Enjoy!
Rebecca Mabry

A **News-Gazette** Book

by Rebecca Mabry
with photos by Vanda Bidwell

Vanda Bidwell

The News-Gazette®

EDITOR AND PUBLISHER   John Foreman
PROJECT EDITOR   Amy Eckert
EXECUTIVE EDITOR   John Beck
MANAGING EDITOR   Dan Corkery
PHOTO EDITOR   Darrell Hoemann

Vanda Bidwell
Mike Goebel
Aviva Gold
Meg Thilmony
Tim Mitchell

Front cover photo by Vanda Bidwell, The News-Gazette.
Cover and book design by Aviva Gold, The News-Gazette.
Photos for the chapter entitled '… in your conduct be friendly toward everyone …'
by Tracy Boulian, Naples (Fla.) News

Soft cover ISBN: 978-0-9798420-1-6

Printed in the United States of America.

The News-Gazette, Inc.
15 Main Street
Champaign, IL 61820
Phone: (217) 351-5252
Fax: (217) 351-5245
www.news-gazette.com

THE MOST IMPORTANT LESSON *I learned from the Amish is how to put family above all the clutter and distractions in one's life. This book is dedicated to my important and essential people—all of whom have the last name Mabry. Michael D, Matt and Tammie, Tim and Jan, and Samantha and Charlie.*

Editor's note

It's been nearly 20 years since The News-Gazette first sent reporter Rebecca Mabry to get to know the Amish of East Central Illinois. It was not a trivial assignment. While the Illinois Amish had been a fixture in the rural areas of Douglas and Moultrie counties for well over a century, almost nothing of substance had been published about their faith, their lifestyle or their curious desire to remain "separate" from the dominant culture that surrounded them.

The Amish were a curiosity for passers-by and an attraction for tourists who would increasingly descend on the area each summer. The visitors caught a few glimpses of the odd-looking folk with serious visages and quaint bonnets or beards traveling about the country roads in buggies or turning over the earth with horse plows as if they were somehow locked in the century when they first arrived from farther east.

But the Amish, so set against change, actually were changing rapidly. Even strong backs and horses could no longer support a growing community from the rich, black land alone. The Amish had skills beyond the ability to turn the soil with walk-behind plows. Their handcrafted wood cabinets and home-cooked bread, pies and jams were coveted for kitchens beyond their own, and the Amish, it seemed, were born businessmen.

But if their economy was evolving, their core values were not. The Amish culture, Mabry reported, all turned around their understandings about faith. It wasn't electricity or automobiles they feared, but the connections those contrivances created to a world less centered on faith and family than their own. Their fashions and their lifestyles simply reflected their ideas about the Godliness of humility. And by evolving around the edges—using telephones for business, for example, but never in the home—they could keep the core of their beliefs intact and unthreatened. They could be in the outside world without being "of" it.

Mabry's extraordinary series of stories—developed over the course of months spent trying to understand the Amish—was first published in November 1989 and later republished in booklet form for additional distribution. Nearly two decades later, it was still being sought out as the definitive work on the Illinois Amish.

So when Mabry returned to work as an editor at The News-Gazette after some years' absence, the decision to update and expand her unique original work seemed obvious. For the better part of another year, she exercised both her patience and her uncanny ability to empathize with her subjects to gain unprecedented access to more of the lives, homes and stories originating in "Amish country."

The remarkable work that results separates myth from reality, answering every question a reader or visitor is ever apt to raise about a mysterious and still misunderstood collection of our neighbors here in central Illinois.

As I wrote back in 1989, one of a newspaper's missions is to help us understand one another. I think you'll end up agreeing that few writers have succeeded more admirably in just such an endeavor.

John Foreman
Editor and Publisher
The News-Gazette

Foreword

As a youngster I remember driving with my parents through the local Amish community a time or two and being flooded with questions I wanted to ask. Why are all the curtains blue? Why do the girls wear little white caps? Do they have indoor plumbing or outhouses?

Then in 1989 I spent three months meeting with Amish families for a three-part series I wrote for The News-Gazette called "Be Ye Separate," and I learned the curtains are blue because they like that color, though they need to be plain and without ruffles and frills. I learned the women and little girls wear white caps because of a verse in 1 Corinthians that talks about head coverings. And I learned that their homes have the same plumbing, showers and flushing toilets as modern homes. The Amish even have gas-powered refrigerators.

But even after three months I left with questions and curiosity about their way of life and faith. I kept in touch with several of the Amish families through the years, writing letters and stopping in for visits, and I frequently took friends down to shop in the community. So when the opportunity arose to take another, longer look at the Amish community, I leapt at the chance to renew acquaintances and learn more.

My longtime friend, Vanda Bidwell, a photo technician and photographer at The News-Gazette for more than 25 years, wanted to take the pictures. So the two of us logged hundreds of miles as we spent more than 15 months traveling the roads in the Arcola, Arthur, Sullivan and Atwood communities.

We talked to more than 100 individuals and ate more whoopie pies, fried chicken and homemade bread with apple butter than we should have, but we learned much. We are delighted to share what we learned with you.

Vanda's job was at times the most frustrating because we often would be talking with adorable freckle-faced Amish children, their eyes peeking out from under straw hats and bonnets, riding little ponies or driving carts. These tantalizing images for a photographer never got taken out of her respect for their desire not to be photographed at close range.

All of the photographs were taken at a distance without the Amish people posing. Though some myths exist, such as the one about Amish people believing the camera captures their souls, the simple answer is their church rules forbid them from posing. Many Amish people and some church leaders say they aren't offended if pictures are snapped from a distance while they are driving a horse and buggy or walking down the road or plowing a field. They do object to cameras stuck in their faces, especially when they've asked that their pictures not be taken.

The two of us became adept at long-distance photography, though we never felt comfortable with it. We talked about the photo challenges with many Amish men and women we interviewed and learned that at their get-togethers it's often a topic of conversation—the latest story about another "English" person hanging out a car window clicking pictures—and some are more tolerant of it than others.

But most importantly, we hope this book resolves some of the mysteries about the Amish and that it shows that the people in the plain clothes are, first of all, committed Christians. Their lifestyles serve to keep their lives simple and uncluttered so they can focus on their faith. They struggle with the same challenges other families face, but they find their solutions most often in the fragile pages of their well-worn family Bibles, and in the strength of their brothers and sisters and aunts and uncles and cousins and neighbors.

Their culture is unique. Their hopes and fears and weaknesses are no different from mine or yours. And they are fascinating. They are the Amish of Illinois' Heartland.

Author Rebecca Mabry (left) and Vanda Bidwell.

Lizzie Miller Otto's long, thin hands, folded gently together, bore witness to the 96 years, 1 month and 19 days she'd lived and worked as an Amish housewife, the mother of 12 babies.

The second of those babies died at 3 months of age, likely breaking Lizzie's heart for the first time. But not the last. She waded through the weeks and months following the tragic death of her 67-year-old husband Rudy, who was killed chopping a tree in the woods. She buried one grandson, great-grandchildren, three brothers and a sister. She stood by to help two of her own daughters bury husbands, and she faced endless days and nights in the last months of her life, bedridden and helpless in a daughter's living room.

In her 96 years, Lizzie Otto never desired nor achieved fame nor wealth nor any special status in the Amish community. She commited her life to being a good daughter, a good wife and a good mother. That, her 217 direct descendants say, she did achieve. In her lifetime, she witnessed the transformation of her small Amish community grow from a few hundred into more than 4,000. And though her father farmed, her husband farmed and had a butcher shop for a while, in her last years she saw most of her sons work in businesses or shops to feed their families.

Despite the changes, the constant had been Lizzie Otto's faith. A faith so strong that it spilled onto everything she did and the way she thought about life, the things she needed and didn't need. She believed one has to be ready at any moment to meet God and be deemed worthy of entering heaven. She and her family prayed every morning, sometimes studying Scripture and singing hymns. She prayed each night before bed, and she and Rudy prayed with their children before *and* after every meal.

And she followed the literal interpretations of the Bible she'd been taught by her Amish parents, keeping her head covered with organdy head coverings or black bonnets, never cutting her hair, never being showy nor prideful nor disobedient. She hitched a horse to a buggy to run to the store to get more sugar or coffee, passed on the road by women whose religion didn't preclude them from owning cars. But the horses and buggies kept Lizzie and Rudy tied to their little community in the heartland of Illinois. The horses kept them among like-minded Amish neighbors and family. The horses kept their world small, set apart from those whose faith wasn't as focused on eternity. The couple lived without electricity so their children would not be exposed to worldly temptations through radio and music and television.

And they didn't just live in their community, they were actively involved in the lives of their neighbors and friends, sharing ice cream and cake on birthdays, joining in family work days, jumping in to help when times got tough.

So it's likely Lizzie wouldn't have been surprised had she known that hours after her death in the pre-dawn hours of Aug. 14, 2007, hundreds in her community dropped what they were doing and came together for her and her family. By early

evening that day, after the coffin had been placed on simple, wooden sawhorses, the community began to pour in to pay its respects.

One could hear the steady clip-clopping of scores of horses trotting the country roads, pulling buggies and families toward the home place where Lizzie and Rudy had raised their family. During the day, a large tent had been set up and filled with wooden benches from the church wagons and a metal shed had been emptied, scrubbed and filled with benches and battery-operated fans.

The coffin had been placed inside the door to the shed, with the lid removed for viewing. In keeping with Amish tradition, the wood coffin was bare, with no flowers or potted plants or ribbons nearby. Lizzie wore a black dress and white organdy cape and apron, her white head covering, not much different from other Amish women dressed for burial.

At evening, the line of friends and neighbors and extended family wound through the yard, down a drive and snaked around a vegetable garden. As the line increased, Lizzie's 11 children and their spouses took seats in a row of metal folding chairs inside the shed, facing each other, and the line of visitors walked through the row of family shaking hands, but not stopping to talk except for a few very brief exchanges. A paper plate tacked to the wall admonished: "Please Keep The Line Moving."

Many of her 46 grandchildren, 150 great-grandchildren and 10 great-great-grandchildren, plus their spouses and children, filled other chairs inside the shed. They fanned themselves in the mid-80s heat with plastic lids from ice cream tubs. School-age children, barefoot but dressed in their Sunday clothes, played on a swing set and chased around the yard. Clusters of Amish men and women stood under the large shade trees, likely catching up on family news, wondering if rain was coming or talking of the tomatoes that still needed to be put up. The younger ones might not have personally known Lizzie, but they worked with or were acquainted with her children or grandchildren.

The second full day of the wake began with horses and buggies pulling into the grass pasture at about 10 a.m. In all, more than 2,000 people came through the line to pay their last respects over the two days, a typical crowd for a wake in this tight-knit community.

Many women arrived with casseroles, noodles, sliced meats, salads and baked goods. Young Amish girls in white aprons placed the bowls and pans in a rented refrigeration trailer. Neighbor ladies and family friends took charge of the meals for the family. Neighbors and friends had helped empty and scrub the shed and string long metal ropes between farm equipment for the hundreds of horses and buggies to be tied in the pasture. The women and men in the Amish community had done such preparations for funerals and weddings so many times they needed little direction. They just show up, one minister said, rarely needing an invitation.

At about 6 p.m., the traffic picked up. More than 100 horses stood hitched to their buggies in the pasture, and more still came. A cool breeze from the south began to blow in as an Amish man laid hymnals on the benches in the tent.

At dusk, the young folk began pulling their buggies into the grass pasture, now parking lot. Clean-shaven young men—signifying that they are not married—dressed in dark dress pants and white shirts emerged and assembled in the barn and yard. Young single women, wearing their Sunday dresses and white head coverings, assembled in the pasture.

Then, just before 8, as the clouds reflected the pink and lavender of sunset, some 300 young men and women filed into the tent and filled the rows of wooden benches. Without cue, the boys' deep voices and the girls' sopranos blended as they began to serenade Lizzie's family with a slow German hymn. The receiving line and viewing ended as the music filled the tent. The family turned their chairs to face the young singers and soak up the song and breeze.

"Yes, we'll gather at the river, The beautiful, the beautiful river," promised the second song. "Gather with the saints at the river That flows by the throne of God."

Some songs were in German and some blended German stanzas and English choruses. When the young folk had sung their last song an hour later, an Amish man, speaking in German, stood and spoke for the family, thanking them for the songs that had helped them in their sorrow. He read Lizzie's obituary and then called for all to join in prayer. Everyone turned and knelt, faces to the benches, while he talked about salvation and recited the Lord's Prayer.

Then under the light of the propane lamps hanging from the tent poles, the young people rose and left, one row at a time, walking past the family and past Lizzie's coffin. The remaining visitors did the same, walking past the family and coffin before leaving for the evening in the black of night.

The next morning, horses and buggies and a few cars brought some 600 family and friends to the funeral service. Similar to a Sunday church service, it was conducted entirely in German. A young minister's sermon urged the mourners to get their lives right with the Lord, for they might not be fortunate enough to live to be 96 years old. He reminded them they needed to be ready every minute of every day to face the Lord for judgment.

A bishop, a brother of one of Lizzie's daughters-in-law, spoke about salvation and loving God and living in God's ways.

The service did not eulogize Lizzie, since the Amish hold that all praise goes to God and not individuals, but her local minister read her obituary again.

After the service, the mourners filed past the coffin while a chorus of six Amish couples sang hymns. The coffin was placed inside coffinmaker Obadiah Helmuth's buggy for the trip to Otto Cemetery, which sits off the County Line Road south of Arthur.

The caravan of buggies was ranked in descending order from the oldest child to the youngest. Other family buggies and cars followed behind as the sky thundered and a light rain fell.

After more prayer at the cemetery, family and friends looked at Lizzie's life-worn body one last time, and then the four pallbearers set the coffin into a rough pine box and lowered it into the grave. As the four men filled the grave, the Amish couples sang more hymns. Some grandchildren participated by ceremoniously adding a shovelful of dirt to the grave, a final effort to do one last thing for their grandma.

The wind picked up, and as the mourners left the cemetery, the sky dumped rain as the buggies pulled away. One of Lizzie's daughters-in-law said she thought God had a hand in holding back the rain that morning. Lizzie's grave is next to her husband, and in time it will be marked with a plain white stone the same size and shape as all the others there. But her family will tell you that her soul is now resting in Paradise.

After 96 years, 1 month and 19 days on this Earth, living the life of a good Christian woman preparing for eternity, Lizzie Miller Otto has received her heavenly reward.

Through her nine decades in the community, she saw Amish life change as the families switched from farming to woodworking to make their livings.

She saw an increasing number of non-Amish people driving through the community and stopping by the farms. Some of the passers-by and tourists might have even seen Lizzie in her buggy. Or working in her garden. Or walking to the barn with a propane lamp. The tourists might have thought she lived without electricity and drove a horse and buggy because she loved the past so much she wanted to live in it.

But her Amish lifestyle had nothing to do with loving the past.

The Amish way of life that Lizzie and her people have chosen is not about looking backward or reclaiming days gone by. Every minute of a good Amish man's or woman's life is spent doing exactly the opposite—looking forward to eternity. The path the Amish have chosen is fraught with rules and restrictions to help them get there, made tolerable and comfortable to most by the strong family ties and traditions.

And so when a frail little Amish lady reaches the end of her life, she doesn't die alone, unnoticed. In the cool of an evening, 300 teenagers and young adults will raise their voices to sing about gathering at that beautiful river. And more than 2,000 men and women will show up to pay tribute.

Being Amish is not about the past.

It's about family. It's about faith.

And most of all, it's about reaching that beautiful shore.

'Pray every day, falling upon your knees'

–from the Amish Rules of a Godly Life

Early in the dark of morning, long before dawn, Ben and Betty Graber gather five of their children together in the basement kitchen of their farmhouse. The light from the propane gas lamp overhead casts stark shadows as they gather and kneel and, speaking in Pennsylvania Dutch, say a prayer of worship and thanksgiving to God. Ben's voice then leads them in a slow German hymn, and this day, Ben follows it by reading a sad story about a child who had been mocked and teased at school. On the days when their father doesn't read a lesson story, the children—Aden, 22, Brandon, 20, Marcus, 14, Marty, 12, and Darlene, 10—take turns reading Bible stories out loud.

As breakfast is put on the table, but before they eat, the children and their parents pray again. Then after the meal they say thanks to God for their blessings once more. All is accomplished before Aden, Brandon and Ben leave for work at 5:30. The younger children help clean up breakfast dishes, curry the pony and hitch him to the cart for the two-mile drive to their country parochial school. On Saturdays and Sundays, the family might rise a little later, but again the prayers are said, hymns sung.

Setting aside this time for worship each morning—seven days a week no matter what—is what the Amish call their family or daily devotions. Nearly every Amish home has a similar ritual of joining together, kneeling, bowing their heads in prayer and singing a hymn or two. It is such an important ritual they arrange their lives around it.

The Grabers rise each morning at 4:15 so they can have the 15 to 20 minutes for devotions and breakfast. Most Amish families bow their heads and pray silently before their meals; and after each meal, more prayers. And most families make time before bed for prayers, maybe family singing, and if there are children, Bible stories. Their Bibles often bear witness to daily use. One church leader's Bible, worn thin from his workman's hands rifling daily through its delicate pages, is held together with strips of duct tape and marked in the margins with hundreds of ink notations.

Though a changing farm economy toppled their longstanding tradition of making their livings off the land, the time they make in their lives for daily devotions is the rock-solid foundation that keeps the Amish—Amish. Fewer than 15 percent of the young people in the community decide against becoming members of the church, so scores of young men and women are baptized each year. The Amish population in the Arthur-Arcola area is flourishing.

Illinois' Arthur-Arcola community is the ninth-largest Amish settlement in North America, according to Donald Kraybill, a nationally recognized scholar on Anabaptist groups and a professor at Elizabethtown College in Pennsylvania. Some 3,000 to 4,000 Amish live in Moultrie-Douglas counties, extending as far southwest as Sullivan and also into Coles County, east to Arcola, as far north as Atwood and Garrett, and to a distance 5 to 6 miles west of Arthur.

The population has nearly doubled since 1990, when 2,400 Amish lived in the area. In 1953, the number was 800.

And the settlement in Moultrie-Douglas counties is no longer the only one in the state. Since 1990, there have been 18 new Amish settlements created, mostly in western and southern Illinois.

Hammond · Atwood · Tuscola · Douglas County · Lovington · Arthur · Moultrie County · Arcola · Cooks Mills · Sullivan · Coles County

Though farming doesn't support the majority of families, the economy hums to the sounds of air-powered sanders and saws as their woodworking and cabinet shops, pallet and truss-building and cottage industries contribute some $100 million a year to the local economy. Unemployment is zero. In fact, the Amish shops have so many job openings, they fill some with non-Amish. It's not unusual in the summertime to see Mexican immigrants walking or riding bikes home to Arcola after spending a day in an Amish cabinet shop.

And at the end of the lanes leading to most Amish farms are signs selling goods or services—potatoes, tree removal, wind chimes.

The Amish community in the Arthur-Arcola area is unique among the large settlements because it is old, dating back to 1865, and it remains isolated in the rural countryside, unlike some of the Amish communities in Ohio and Pennsylvania that are being surrounded by sprawling cities.

Pioneers Moses Yoder, Daniel Miller and Daniel Otto brought their families to Arthur in 1865 from Summit Mills, Pa., buying land for $8.10 an acre. The town of Arthur didn't exist then, but today, hundreds of people passing through the town drive past the pioneer Amish cemetery that sits alongside Illinois 133, across the street from Yoder's Kitchen.

Other families moved in from Ohio, Indiana, Iowa and Pennsylvania, and by 1888, the settlement had grown so large they needed to divide into two church districts. Today there are 27.

The Amish hold their church services in homes, so they keep the number of families in a church district small—about 25. That means 100 to 150 people might

"Sunday is a day of rest, light meal, light work. If the hay's ready on Saturday, it can wait until Monday. Sunday is the day to stay together as a family for church, for worship." —Amish bishop

show up at a home for a Sunday church service, and in Amish circles that's a manageable crowd. The small church districts maintain a closeness among members because they're all living in the same rural neighborhoods. The church leaders in each district live down the road or across the section. "You know everybody," a bishop said. "We see them every two weeks for church and we also neighbor with them. If there's something going on in the neighborhood they're part of it and we're part of it. We see them all the time."

"(Our children) don't know anything except to go to church. They go to church from the time they're four weeks old." —Amish minister

The Amish strongly believe God has a hand in their lives, and He can see the goodness—and weakness—in their hearts. So all of the church leaders are chosen by lots, believing that this lets God make the decision. They base this on the Biblical description of Matthias being selected to replace Judas as one of the apostles in Acts. In each church district there is one bishop, two ministers and one deacon. The Amish church leaders serve for life once they are selected, unless ill health forces retirement. And the ceremony in which a man is selected is sacred and time-honored. The men and women in the district, without talking about it among themselves, consider a man who they think would make a good leader.

And on the Sunday when the selection is made, each member will nominate by whisper the name of a man to the church leaders.

All men who receive multiple votes are candidates. The number of candidates ranges from several to a dozen or more. A corresponding number of hymnals are laid on a long table, each one bound together with a rubber band. The men choose a hymnal in order of their ages, from oldest to the youngest. Inside one of the hymnals is a piece of paper containing the verse from Acts 1:24 that says, "Thou Lord which knoweth the hearts of men, shew whether of these thou has chosen to this ministry." The man is then asked to stand before the bishop, who then tells him his specific duties and gives him best wishes in the name of Jesus Christ.

"To accept it is the will of God," the bishop said.

Asked about a young Amish boy who might grow up yearning to be a minister but never picks the right hymnal, a bishop shook his head. "That might be his cross that he will have to bear," he said. "We all have things we have to accept sometimes, and that might be his—his cross to bear."

A new minister is mentored by the experienced ministers but doesn't receive formal training. "The church has a tendency to go easy on (a new minister) for a year or so," a bishop said. "But they are expected to jump in and learn."

When young men join the church, one question they are asked is if they will be willing to serve as minister. So it is a responsibility most men consider in their lifetimes. Some are ordained in their 50s, but many are in their 20s. Several in the Arthur-Arcola area have been ordained as young as 22.

The bishop, the two ministers and the deacon in each district have distinct responsibilities.

"The bishop is considered the leader," said one bishop. "He's not the boss, he's the leader. There's a difference." Bishops marry couples and bishops baptize. As leaders of their districts, all the bishops meet once or twice a year to talk about issues in the community. But there is no central overseer of the church districts. Each district makes its own rules, though it would be rare for one district's rules to be much different from a neighboring district within the same community.

The deacons oversee the church district's finances, like a treasurer, and because the Amish do not have health insurance the deacon also helps families if they need it with medical bills. The Amish don't tithe a certain percentage of their income, but they are generous with their contributions to their church district's treasury. The deacon is also the one who makes the first visit to a family if they are doing something that is against church rules. "The deacon is the one who goes to help the guy see the error of his ways and help him to mend his ways," a bishop said. "But he doesn't do it without counsel (of the bishop and minister)."

Amish settlements can be found in 24 states and Ontario, Canada. The population of children and adults is estimated at 150,000.

The minister's main focus is on preparing for the Sunday worship service, in which he might be called on to present either the short (30-minute) sermon or the longer one that can go on an hour to an hour-and-a-half.

Three bishops sat for an interview for this book, but because they preach to their members to not grab attention, the three did not want to be identified. Each one has several decades of leadership, and each sat for about two hours to explain some of the basic principles of their faith. They understand the curiosity about their lifestyles and religion, and they want the information to be accurate. But as one said, the Amish don't like spotlights or stages. They like uniformity. They are not interested in opportunities for individualism that could lead to one-upmanship. That's why women don't wear buttons on their dresses or jewelry or barrettes. Those kind of adornments aren't needed and could lead to one woman having nicer, prettier buttons than the other women. That's why all the men's hats are alike, why all buggies are the same and don't have a little chrome here or there, and why the houses are white, without shutters. Their focus is to be on their faith and their families, not on trying to make impressions.

And the Amish live by a set of rules that change very slowly, if at all.

The rules the Amish live by are called the Ordnung, which is German for order, and they are not written in a book. The obvious ones forbid using public electricity or owning a vehicle, and they set dress codes and require the use of horses and buggies for transportation. Married men wear beards, girls and women keep their heads covered, and the children do not go to school after eighth grade.

From state to state and Amish community to Amish community, variations of the rules occur. In Pennsylvania, buggies can be gray, but must be black in Illinois. Likewise in Pennsylvania, Amish men wear their hats into the church service and remove them before the service begins; Illinois Amish men remove their hats before entering a house.

The colors that the Illinois Amish women choose for their dresses are always solid colors and most often dark shades of blue, green, burgundy and gray. The styles and hemlines and necklines are very similar and are made from patterns generations old. No creativity is allowed in finishing dresses—no fancy stitching, rick-rac or other garnishment.

"We don't like showy or loud," one bishop explained. "Anything that draws attention."

And what's wrong with drawing attention to yourself?

The bishop wrinkled his brow. "Well, why would you want to?"

"Why not stay with something that's practical and simple?" he asked. "You don't have to be different from your neighbor. We're trying to maintain a uniformity.

Married Amish men wear untrimmed beards on their jawlines; single men are clean-shaven.

The rich don't look different from the poor." So the Amish purses and shoes are plain black. The men and boys all wear homemade denim breeches; most men wear black leather suspenders. Parents cut their little boys' hair so that it's short on the sides and all one length—a cut the boys wear into manhood. There's no room for crewcuts or ponytails.

The bishops said they try to encourage their people to ask the question: How does my decision look to God? "Ask, Is this what I should be doing?"

The rules and restrictions keep some positive statistics in the district. The Amish do not approve of divorce, and a divorced couple cannot remarry. The divorce rate among the Amish is very low; in the Amish parochial schools, few of the children come from broken homes.

The melodies of the Amish hymns are not recorded with notes on paper but are passed down orally from generation to generation.

"One reason that we don't have that many divorces in our Amish churches is that we don't consider it an option," said a bishop. "We don't believe the Bible leaves that as an option, so our children grow up with that impression. And I think that has a bearing on them being careful about who they choose for a partner. And they realize that if they have problems they're going to have to work them out. Some get worked out and some don't. There are some marriage problems."

Counseling is available, and the community has annual marriage meetings that routinely draw 150 couples or more. They talk about the kinds of issues that help marriages become strong: the man being a good Christian leader of the household, and the woman being a partner but submitting to the husband's final decision. And the focus of the family is to be raising the children to be good Christians and good Amish men and women.

Having those family devotions each morning, like Ben and Betty Graber and thousands of other Amish families, is the key to instilling that desire in the young. "We were brought up by our parents to be Amish," Ben said. "The whole idea is, we teach by example."

CHURCH SERVICE

The Amish in Illinois have no church houses. The families take turns holding church in their homes for the 25 to 30 families in their church district. Some families hold church in their scrubbed-out sheds, shops or barns.

There are 27 church districts in the Arthur-Arcola area. Each church district meets for church every other Sunday. On the off-Sunday, people often attend church in a relative's district.

Each church district has a deacon who serves as treasurer, two ministers who take turns delivering sermons, and a bishop who is the leader. There is no central authority in the Amish church, and each of the 230-some Amish settlements in North America are their own entities with their own rules and regulations. Some communities are more liberal about issues. For example, the community in Kalona, Iowa, allows farming with tractors. Others are more conservative and will not allow the use of gas-powered equipment, like lawn mowers. Local "rules" are called the Ordnung, and though they are not written down, they are rarely changed without consensus from all the bishops in a community. One such change in the Arthur-Arcola community allowed the use of bicycles.

The women sit together, the married women in the front rows and the single women to the back. Very young children sit with both their mothers and fathers.

A few days before a family hosts church, women relatives and neighbors will arrive to help the homemaker wash windows and give the house a thorough cleaning. Furniture is moved to a back room to clear the house for the service.

Many of the Amish homes have wooden interior walls that can be raised and hooked to the ceiling or folded away to make their home one big meeting room for the 100 to 125 who attend the Sunday morning service.

Each church district has its own church wagon, which holds wooden benches, hymnals, a few folding chairs, dishes, plastic water glasses, silverware and tablecloths. The church districts also borrow church wagons to accommodate the typically large funerals and weddings.

Children of all ages, as young as infants, sit on the wooden benches for the 2- to 3-hour church service. Some parents will take crying infants out but toddlers as young as 2 and 3 occupy themselves with small toys, handkerchiefs and treats like raisins. Older parishioners might sit in folding chairs.

The men sit at one side for the church service, the clergy and the oldest in the front row. The young and unmarried men sit in the back rows. Men often greet the clergy on Sunday mornings with a kiss on the lips, called a "Holy Kiss."

There is no piano or other musical instruments used at a service. The entire service and hymns are in High German, which is standard German. The first language of the Amish is called Pennsylvania Dutch, a dialect of German frequently sprinkled with English. Though the Amish speak the Dutch as their primary language, the services are restricted to High German.

The first two hymns in an Amish church service are slow and can take a total of 30 to 35 minutes. A man selected for his voice, called a Vorsinger, sings the first syllable of a line and then the others join in. They all sing the same tune and there is no harmony. The Vorsinger sets the tempo and key.

The Amish do not address their ministers or bishops with titles, such as pastor or reverend. All clergy are men and they are not paid. They serve for life and hold other jobs.

The Amish hymns come from a book called the Ausbund, and many songs date back to the 1600s, when the Anabaptists were persecuted in Germany and Switzerland. The second hymn is always "Lob Lied" (Praise Him), which begins "O Gott Vater, wir loben dich," "O God Father, we do praise thee."

The first minister preaches for about 30 minutes. There is a lengthy prayer, at which time the Amish turn and kneel, their faces to the benches. After prayer, the deacon reads Scripture while the congregation stands. The second sermon can take an hour or more. The ministers may be visiting from another district or out of state. The bishop, ministers and deacon meet while the first hymns are being sung to determine who will preach. The second sermon is followed with a prayer. The service ends with a hymn.

"The church wagon holds everything except the preacher." –Amish minister

'In the name of the Father, Son & Holy Spirit...'

One summer day just after noon, when some Amish put their feet up and take a little snooze, a horse and buggy pulled up at an Amish cemetery south of Arthur. David D. Schrock stepped out from the buggy and grabbed a gallon of white-silver paint and a paint brush. He pointed out that he'd gotten the paint for a good price at a local store, and it came with a 25-year guarantee.

Yoder Cemetery sits back in a field 100 yards or so, with a grassy lot separating it from the road. All the white stones are the same size and shape, and contain the same basic dates in keeping with the Amish belief that all their people, rich and poor, be equal. Some of the limestone markers date back to the 1880s.

David knelt next to a stone and scrubbed moss away with a wire brush, then laid down a good coat of new paint. And he introduced his family—his mother, Ada Mast Schrock, and his father, Daniel J. Schrock. And over there, his mother's parents, and across there his father's. And then there's the stone for his great-great-grandfather Daniel Schrock—born in 1828, died in 1890—one of the first to migrate from Holmes County, Ohio, to the Arthur-Arcola area.

The story of Daniel Schrock's death more than 100 years ago is well-known in the community and to visitors at the Amish Interpretive Center in Arcola. Daniel Schrock's suit coat is on a mannequin there, alongside a story that tells that while visiting Partridge, Kan., in 1890, he walked over a ravine on a railroad bridge, misstepped and fell to his death.

The story goes that before his body returned home, his dog had been acting strangely. When the casket bearing his master's body returned to the farm, the casket was placed in the yard so the dog could have one last look. The dog fell down, never ate again and soon died.

Each year, Daniel Schrock's descendents borrow his century-old suit coat from the museum for Schrock family reunions.

David painted Daniel Schrock's stone that day, as he did the stones for two former neighbors. They didn't have family locally, he said.

When told he was a good man for looking after all the stones for his family and neighbors, he shook his head. "Nah," he said. "Jesus said, 'No one is good except God alone.'" At 67, David can quote a lot of Scripture; he has been a minister for 43 years. He grew up in the white, two-story house built by his great-grandfather, walked to the same country school that his father and grandfather attended, and farmed the same land. Now, David's son Howard farms it.

And Howard's son, Eldon, 11, mowed the grassy lot at the cemetery as David painted the stones.

The family trees in this Amish community offer much shade for the telling and retelling of family stories. Many have roots that go back to the earliest pioneer settlers with the names of Yoder, Beachy, Miller, Otto, Kauffman, Herschberger, Schrock and Helmuth. The town of Arthur didn't exist back in 1864 when the first Amish scouting party arrived.

Descendants borrow Daniel Schrock's suit coat from the museum for family reunions.

They were Amish men from Pennsylvania and Maryland looking for land in Wisconsin and Missouri, but when passing through Illinois they heard the railroad was selling land near Arcola at a good price—about $8 an acre. They took a train to Mattoon, walked the 15 miles to Arcola and enlisted a local farmer to drive them around in a wagon for a few days.

"We were brought up by our parents to be Amish. We teach by example."
—Ben Graber

In 2004, a memorial was erected on the banks of the Limmat River in Zurich, Switzerland, honoring Felix Manz, who was drowned in 1527 for his part in the Anabaptist movement.

The men liked what they saw, the Amish history says. The two returned to Illinois a few months later, accompanied by two more Amish men. Daniel Miller bought the first property—a farm one mile east of what is now Arthur. And Moses Yoder bought 160 acres located 3.5 miles south and a half mile east of Arthur, according to a history written by D. Paul Miller of Illinois Wesleyan University. In the spring of 1865, just as the Civil War ended, wagonloads of Amish families began arriving from Pennsylvania, Delaware and Ohio to start a new settlement.

In the century before, the earliest Amish immigrants sailed to America, settling first in eastern Pennsylvania, where William Penn promised religious freedom. The spiritual baggage they brought with them included fear and suspicion due to the hundreds of years their people in Switzerland, Austria, Germany and Holland had been tormented and executed.

Three names most every adult Amish knows by heart today are Konrad Grebel, Georg Blaurock and Felix Manz. These three young religious students were living in Zurich, Switzerland, in 1525 when they began to believe in a free church—one not tied to the state—and more importantly in adult baptism. The Roman Catholic Church and government required that all children be baptized within seven days after birth, but these three argued that baptism should be reserved for those old enough to make a personal commitment to God. In a meeting at the home of Felix Manz's mother in the evening of Jan. 21, 1525, they decided to form their own church. It's said that Georg Blaurock jumped up and said, "Konrad, for God's sake baptize me with the true Christian Baptism." Felix Manz brought a bucket of water and the first adult baptisms were performed. Anabaptists, which they were called, means Rebaptism. Within three years, the three were dead. The city government executed Manz by throwing him bound and tied from a boat into the Limmat River in Zurich in May 1527. Executioners tied Blaurock to a stake and burned him alive in 1527.

Grebel died in the plague epidemic the same year. But the deaths of these radical reformists only drove the movement underground. Anabaptists continued to get new members. Between 2,000 and 4,000 Anabaptists were persecuted and martyred between 1527 and 1571 in Switzerland, Holland, Austria and Germany, according to Walter Beachy, a Mennonite minister from Plain City, Ohio, who teaches Anabaptist history.

"They didn't keep official records," Beachy said. "But in all cases, the magistrates deputized people willing to do it and they would be paid so much a head for bringing (the Anabaptists) in, and if they tried to escape they were killed." In 1538, a former Catholic priest named Menno Simons stepped forward to lead the movement and members called themselves Mennonites. But a split in 1690 over the discipline of an erring church member created a division and splinter group for members with more strict philosophies on church discipline. Those members followed Bishop Jacob Ammon and became known as the Amish.

This history dates back 500 years but it is not forgotten among the Amish. At each Sunday church service they sing slow German hymns, frequently written by imprisoned Anabaptists. The history of martyrdom is a common theme in the hymns and studies of Amish groups.

The persecution of the Amish in Europe affected the way they practice their religion today, said Walter Beachy. Since the persecution drove them underground, they lost all interest in evangelical mission work and began to focus on their own families and their own districts. It's true today that the Amish do not seek new members from outside their community. They also met secretly in members' houses, and today most hold the church services in their homes.

No Amish live in Europe today, Beachy said. There are some 230 settlements in North America, including a few in Canada. Some recently tried starting settlements in Belize and other Central American countries.

But it takes a community in order to be Amish. They need to live among other Amish in order to practice their faith and accommodate the required lifestyles. An Amish family couldn't live in a house on Green Street in Champaign, for example, keeping their horse in the garage and traveling by buggy some 40 miles to church. More importantly, it would break the basic rule that requires them to be separate and apart from the world, not in the midst of it.

But they are always reaching out and forming new settlements. In 1990, the Arthur-Arcola community was the only one in Illinois. Now there are 18 Amish communities in the state. Some of the areas with new settlements are Ava, Barry, Cisne, Flat Rock, Macomb, Pittsfield, Robinson and Vienna. Some were started by clusters of families moving together from Ohio, Indiana, Delaware and oth-

The Ausbund hymn book, dating back to the 1500s, is said to be the oldest Christian song book in continuous use.

"We see motherhood as a good thing ... and that it's necessary for the women to stay home and have families." –Bishop

The Amish national weekly newspaper, The Budget, contains news sent in by scribes from 230-some Amish communities. The local weekly newspaper is the Echo.

er Eastern states. And a few have been started by families who moved from the Arthur-Arcola area.

Raising questions about the new settlements with local Amish people seems to touch a raw nerve with some. One bishop said some families moved to southern Illinois near Carbondale to create a new settlement because they wanted a better environment for their children. He said families grew concerned that the local community had become too large and they wanted their children in a more isolated community. Also, land prices are cheaper in southern and western Illinois, so families could afford to get 40 acres for a price that would buy 10 or 20 here.

But some of the Amish families who moved to southern Illinois have created communities called New Order Amish, and while they do use horses and buggies, dress in plain clothes and separate themselves in their own community with their own parochial school, some live with telephones, farm with tractors and have electricity—though they cannot have air conditioning or ceiling fans.

One Amish housewife confided she had family in Ava in southern Illinois and she's OK with it. But when those family members come back to visit in the Arthur-Arcola community, they are not welcomed by all.

A bishop from the Arthur area admitted there is a difference of opinion about the New Order. "There's really no true cut and dried (difference) between Old Order and New Order. A lot of that is a label. Some of our people are more open to these smaller communities than others are."

He said some New Order communities do allow members to have electricity, but not all. "Flat Rock is considered New Order but they don't have electricity. They still use horses and buggies and farm with horses. And there's a new order community at Ava, and they farm with tractors and have electricity in the houses and things like that and they are called New Order but there's some back and forth with this community.

"Kalona, Iowa, is Old Order Amish and they've always farmed with tractors. So it's not cut and dried."

Donald Kraybill, a nationally recognized expert on Anabaptist groups and a professor at Elizabethtown College in Pennsylvania, said the New Order groups do raise concerns with the Old Order Amish. But Kraybill said New Order Amish have lived side-by-side with the Old Order community in Holmes County, Ohio, and seem to be getting along cooperatively. But whenever the New Order are close by, Kraybill said, the Old Order Amish are worried their members will be enticed to leave.

There is no central authority in the Amish religion, so each settlement can make its own Ordnung, or rules. Kraybill said some New Order settlements have Sunday school year-round instead of just in the summer. Some emphasize Bible studies for their youth groups, and some are doing mission work and Christian aid activities.

"The Amish became suspicious of change and decided to freeze their culture and lifestyle. An Amish man today reflects the dress and culture of the first half of the 1800s." –Walter Beachy

The next step closer to modern living in the continuum beyond the Old Order Amish and New Order Amish is that of the Beachy Amish, called the Beachy Mennonites locally. These Mennonites have cars and electricity but no televisions. The women sew their own plain dresses and small white caps similar to Amish women; the men buy their clothes. The Beachy Mennonites attend the Pleasant View Mennonite Church west of Arcola and the Trinity Christian Church in rural Sullivan.

Another conservative group of Mennonites are those who attend the Church of God in Christ, Mennonite. These Mennonites are also known as Holderman Mennonites or in the area, Prairie Mennonites. They live under the guidelines of modesty and simplicity. The women sew their own dresses and are allowed to wear prints. The women also wear black head coverings—a folded head covering worn on the head for everyday wear and a three-cornered head covering tied under the chin for devotional service. The men buy their clothing and wear beards. The Holderman Mennonites use computers for business and the Internet with the use of filters. They do not use radios or televisions, but have cars. The Church of

God in Christ Mennonite church is located about three-and-a-half miles north of Arthur.

There are also the Conservative Mennonites, who worship at the Sunnyside Mennonite Church in rural Arcola and the North Vine Mennonite Church in Arthur. Conservative Mennonite women often wear small lace veils and dress modestly. These members have TVs, radios, cars and other technology. Another conservative branch of the Mennonites, called the Eastern Mennonites, have started a church near Arthur.

The Arthur Mennonite Church does not require head coverings, members dress as they wish, and there are no restrictions on technology.

But despite all the technicalities that differentiate the Mennonite sects and the Amish, they are still lumped together as Anabaptists, and of that entire group the Amish are the fastest growing segment.

"And that's without doing any kind of evangelism or mission work," Walter Beachy said. "Of course, (the Amish) teach strongly against any kind of birth control and to have large families, and they retain a high percentage of their youth." Locally, Amish church leaders say they retain more than 85 percent—maybe as much as 90 percent—of their young people.

The Amish will tell you they bring up their children to be Amish. If it doesn't happen, they are heartbroken.

The young Amish, like young Eldon Schrock mowing at the cemetery while his grandpa David Schrock painted the tombstones, hear their aunts and uncles and cousins tell the stories about their ancestors at family reunions and get-togethers. They see Daniel Schrock's century-old suit coat and hear about his mournful dog. They hear about the martyrdom. And for many, like Eldon when he drives the pony cart, they're traveling the same country roads their great-great-grandfathers traveled. He knows his roots. He and many others are growing up aware of a past.

And some sunny afternoon 20 or 30 years from now, Eldon or one of his siblings or cousins might be the one to drive a buggy around the sections to Yoder Cemetery with a gallon of paint he got at a good price to preserve the Schrock family history.

WHAT DO THE AMISH BELIEVE?

The Amish believe in the holy trinity—God the Father, Jesus and the Holy Spirit—and they live by the Old and New Testament and the Apostles' Creed. They also follow the Dordrecht Confession of Faith, which was adopted by Mennonites in 1632. It outlines, with references to Scripture, the beliefs on such issues as selecting church leaders, marriage, foot washing, Communion, baptism and other church laws and traditions.

> I believe in God, the Father Almighty, maker of Heaven and Earth, and in Jesus Christ our Lord: Who was conceived of the Holy Spirit, born of the Virgin Mary, suffered under Pontius Pilate, was crucified, dead and buried. And the third day, rose from the dead, ascended into heaven and sitteth at the right hand of God, the Father Almighty. From thence he shall come again to judge the quick and the dead. I believe in the Holy Spirit, the Holy Apostolic Church, the communion of Saints, the forgiveness of sins, the resurrection of the body, and life everlasting. Amen.

ADULT BAPTISM

The Amish originated from a religious sect called Anabaptists, which means rebaptized, that arose in Europe in the 16th century. The Anabaptists fiercely refused to give up their belief in adult baptism despite thousands being tortured and killed—often burned alive—by fellow Christians for it. In fact, the pace of most of their German hymns are deliberately slow so they cannot be danced to because in the days of persecution, when Anabaptists were led down the streets to their deaths and bravely sang hymns, the tormentors danced. Most of the hymns the Amish sing in their churches today were written by imprisoned Anabaptists and convey the anguish of the times. This church history is taught to the young people so the price paid by their ancestors is not forgotten. In the Arthur-Arcola community, teenagers need to be about 16 years old in order to be baptized. They receive nine weeks of Sunday instruction. The baptisms follow church services. The young people meet privately with the bishop and ordained men for several minutes to talk about the commitment they are making. Once a young person is baptized, he or she has to obey the laws and rules of the church or face shunning or excommunication. The teens and ministers then return to the congregation, the teens kneel and are baptized by the bishop. The girls remove their head coverings and the bishop places his cupped hand on the applicant's head, then the deacon or minister will pour a little water between the bishop's hands three times for the Father, Son and Holy Spirit. The baptism is not celebrated with gifts or parties but is often an emotional day for parents and grandparents.

BE YE SEPARATE

The Amish have taken a verse from 2 Corinthians that admonishes "be not yoked with unbelievers" and ends with the command, "Come from among them and be ye separate," and made it the framework on which they've built their lives. They do not want to take part in the temptations they believe the devil planted in the world. They deliberately keep their communities the focus of their lives and do not participate in organizations, clubs or causes with non-Amish. They have no interest in politics, Hollywood and fashion or contemporary trends, and they would not pursue hobbies or interests that would take them away from their family and community. This is also why most do not participate in Social Security. They also do not have medical insurance because it would require joining with others who are not Amish. The churches pool money to help families cover medical costs of their members.

Noncombatants

The Amish are pacifists but will serve as conscientious objectors if drafted. During the Vietnam War, several local Amish men served in hospitals.

No posed photos

The Amish have a church ordinance that prohibits them from posing for pictures. Locally, if asked, the Amish will say they are not offended if photos are taken from a long distance without their knowledge. They do object to tourists who rudely stick a camera in their faces, even after being asked not to.

Horses and buggies

Horses and buggies limit the Amish to their own small community. An Amish family cannot go to a Champaign steakhouse in a horse and buggy, but they can go down the road to have birthday cake with a great-uncle. The church leaders made the decision generations ago to ban motor vehicles because they saw automobiles giving people the independence to go out and be part of the world—diluting their interest and time for family and neighbors in their own community. The Amish will ride in cars and routinely hire Amish taxis to go to doctor's appointments and visit relatives in other communities. The Arthur-Arcola community made a decision back in the 1950s to allow male members to drive vehicles so they could work off the farm—but that decision was quickly revoked when church leaders saw it having a negative impact. Most of the Amish tradesmen have non-Amish employees or hired drivers to transport them to work sites; some of the Amish-owned shops and factories hire vans to pick up and deliver their Amish employees who live too far away for commutes with horses and buggies.

No ties to public electricity

The Amish do not run electric lines to their homes, though they will use generators, air compressors, batteries and diesel engines to produce electricity to run machinery or power tools. Some literature says they object to joining the electrical power grid because of their desire to not be joined with unbelievers, but most locally say they do not want electricity in their homes because they want to keep radios, stereos, TVs, computers and video games out and away from their children. Some Amish businesses have used word processors run on generators, and the Amish have no problem using modern tools, like gas-powered lawn mowers, because they are not seen as a threat to their lifestyles and families.

No telephones in the home

The Amish have a strong work ethic and believe that idle chatter over telephones is unproductive and unhelpful. In recent years, Amish families have been allowed cell phones for their businesses but they are not to be brought into their homes. The Amish also have phone shacks, often shared by several neighbors, where a phone with voicemail records messages. The church leaders discourage using the phones for non-business-related calls.

Men are decision-makers

The men are heads of the households and bread-winners. The church leaders teach that the men are to be good leaders in their households and to discuss issues with their wives, but the man is to make final decisions and the woman is to accept and respect his decision. Mothers don't work outside the home. The church leaders discourage married women from working outside the home because the women are expected to sew the family clothes, keep an orderly home and tend large gardens to feed the families through the year. Women with children do not work outside the home because their focus is to be on raising the children and sewing, gardening and homemaking. Amish families typically have four to seven children.

No high school

The Amish place great value on educating their children but will not send them to high school. This is because the Amish believe the eighth-grade education serves them well as farmers and craftsmen, but high school would expose them to temptations in the world. The church leaders say that though the schooling ends at eighth grade, the young teens are educated in the work ethic, life skills, adult responsibilities and in learning trades or homemaking skills by their parents during those high school years.

Prepare for Judgment Day

The Amish strongly believe that every minute of every day one has to be ready to face the Lord. Church leaders encourage members to pray for guidance throughout the day. If women are singing or humming at chores, they are singing church hymns. The local church leaders discourage off-color jokes or cussing, and Amish members are not to drink alcohol, use unprescribed drugs or smoke.

Corporal punishment

Most of the Amish believe in raising their children with a firm hand and that spanking is appropriate to correct misbehavior. Local church leaders are quick to stress that they encourage "warming the bottoms" but no hitting or slapping about the head. The Amish church leaders often address child discipline at their annual marriage meetings. And they encourage parents to have high expectations for behavior and set rules and boundaries for the children, but also to give them a word of encouragement when appropriate. Most do not believe in indulging children with exorbitant gifts—birthdays and Christmas usually yield modest, practical gifts. A 9-year-old boy's Christmas bounty might consist of new winter gloves, a flashlight and a softball bat.

Marry for lifetime

Divorce is rare among the Amish. They believe marriage is a commitment made with God, and the pact can only be broken by death. If a couple does divorce, if there is an "innocent" party that did not disobey the wedding vows and does not sue for divorce, that person would be allowed to remain a member of the church. Widows and widowers can remarry.

The Amish do not like becoming entangled in courts, so they are not allowed to file lawsuits. They pay all the taxes other people pay—real estate, income tax and sales tax. Many do not contribute to Social Security.

Ground travel OK

The Amish do not fly on airplanes except in emergencies but travel by train, bus and rented vans and vehicles. Each winter, busloads of retired Amish from the Northern states head to Pinecraft, an Amish settlement near Sarasota, Fla., to escape the weather.

COMMUNION

The Amish celebrate communion in the Easter season and also in the fall. The church service at communion time lasts about six hours, although members take turns leaving one at a time for a light refreshment while the preaching continues. The Amish bishops serve homemade bread and communal cups of red wine, and members also participate in foot washing at these special times. They pair up man to man and woman to woman and take turns kneeling and washing each other's feet. The practice comes from John 13:1-17 in which Jesus washed the feet of his apostles following the last supper. It is to remind members of the importance of humility and of being clean and pure before Christ.

SHUNNING

The act of shunning a member of the faith who breaks the rules is considered a last resort and is not often done, according to a local minister. But if an Amish church member, for example, purchased a piece of modern equipment clearly not allowed by the church, the man would receive multiple visits from the church leaders and possibly many family members. And if he refused to get rid of the offending equipment, the other Amish would no longer associate with him. And it could lead to his excommunication.

But the young people who do not join the Amish church are not shunned because they are not breaking the rules of the church, which apply only to baptized members. If Amish church members who have been baptized decide later to leave the church, they are also not shunned for their decision, though families will say it is heartbreaking for all involved.

"We have certain Scriptures announced two weeks ahead—but the minister has wide latitude. He can speak about whatever he wants." –Bishop

'Observe the Sabbath and keep it holy'

–from Rules of a Godly Life

T**o the Amish, church services are a reverent, sacred time. Many say they look forward to church all week.**

They don't often include outsiders, so I felt privileged to be able to join a friend. I gave a lot of thought to how I should dress so as not to offend and ended up picking a long, black skirt, black stockings, black shoes and a dark, long-sleeved shirt. I didn't wear jewelry other than my watch and wedding ring.

I knew the entire service would be in High German, which is what the Amish call the standard German language, so I took my own Bible to read and study so I would not be gawking and staring.

The Amish hold church services in their homes or cleaned-up outbuildings, and this Sunday the services were being held in a large, metal workshop beside the home. When we arrived, clusters of men stood outside the shed talking in low voices or whispers, if at all. And once inside, the men and women, many with young children at their sides and on their laps, did not visit with neighbors. Each seemed deep in personal thought in the quiet. The workshop had been emptied and the cement floors scrubbed. Blue tarps hid the equipment and tools that couldn't be removed. Horses had been unhitched and put in the barn.

Amish homes are built with interior walls that fold up or are raised and hooked to the ceiling to accommodate the large groups for church.

"Our first priority is the children in our house. It's number one."
—Bishop

Many families walked the mile or two to their neighbor's for church rather than come in horse and buggy. On that hot June morning, it presented a striking picture—the men in their black trousers and vests and white shirts and the women in their dark Sunday best dresses with white capes and aprons. Many of the women and children walked barefoot on the roads as they do so often in the summertime. When the music began at 9 a.m., one man, called the Vorsinger or song leader, sang the first syllable or word of each line and then the others joined in. The first two hymns, sung very slowly, took a total of about 35 minutes. They used small, black hymnals but some knew the hymns by heart.

I'd never heard anything like an Amish hymn. It's nearly impossible to find a recording of it because the Amish do not want it recorded. Some music professionals say the Amish songs sound like Gregorian chants. They do not sing in harmony, but the blend of the men's bass and tenor voices with the soprano of the women turned out a beautiful, if sad, hymn that filled the big, metal shed. I could not understand a word, but I understood from their faces that the words were heartfelt.

As the service wore on for about two-and-a-half hours, I became intrigued with the behavior of the young children, some no more than 2 or 3 years old. One little girl kept herself entertained by folding and unfolding a little hankie and looking in a small picture book. I don't recall that she made a peep. A platter of homemade cookies was passed midway for the little ones. When the service ended, all the worshippers—maybe 80 to 90—were invited into the house for a light noon meal. Some of the men stayed behind to pack the hymnbooks into homemade wooden boxes for the church wagon, a long, low wagon that is transported from house to house for the church services. The wagon holds the long, wooden benches with legs that fold up and everything else needed for the day. A minister once joked that the church wagon holds everything but the preacher.

Sundays in an Amish community are devoted to worship and family. They strictly avoid working on the Sabbath Day. The men will do light chores to tend to livestock, and the women will fix light meals. Even if the hay's been cut and a rain's

The light meal served after church includes homemade bread and a peanut butter spread made of creamy peanut butter, marshmallow cream and corn syrup.

blowing in, the hay stays in the field. The noon meal served after church is a traditional one in the community—prepared in advance and light enough to require little cleanup.

The men filed into the basement to eat, sitting at their own tables; the women followed and sat at the others. Some wooden benches had been stacked on top of each other and doubled to make tables covered with white plastic. We sat on the long, wooden benches and helped ourselves to a tasty meal. Every table had recycled margarine bowls variously filled with a peanut butter-marshmallow cream spread, a softened Velveeta cheese spread, slices of homemade bread, lettuce and radishes from the garden, and sweetened banana chunks, all to share. Helpers served fresh coffee and hot tea and water. Of course, all joined in silent prayer before and after the meal. Later, some stayed and visited with the hosts while others went home to rest or went to visit other family.

Sunday afternoons and evenings in the Amish community are traditionally the social times for the young folk, as they're called. Teenage boys 16 years and older will gather to play softball, often at the Otto Center or more recently behind the Arthur High School. Some teenage girls—also 16 or older—go to watch; some teens gather to play volleyball. (Until they are 16, Amish teens are not allowed to run with friends or attend social gatherings without their parents.)

"The whole idea is to stay at the level of your neighbor, and for there to be unity."
–Bishop

Some people hosting church will invite the young folk to come to their home on Sunday evening for a sing. Sometimes, 50 to 75 teenagers will come and share a light supper and sing for a couple of hours.

Later, as I thought about the experience in an Amish church service, I realized the thing that stood out for me is that while I was welcome, no one there had any interest in me. I'd attended a lot of different church services through the years and there's always an interest in attracting a new member. There's always an invitation to come back. Or more. But the Amish don't proselytize. An Amish minister once stated the obvious: it's not easy to convert to Amish. The language is a barrier, and even if one can speak German and Pennsylvania Dutch, few would be able to give up modern living for the Amish rules and restrictions. And the Amish don't seek to grow their religion with outsiders. They tend it and care for it within their own ranks. So they welcomed me as an invited guest, and I appreciated the honesty of it. I respect the importance they placed on the day, and am still amazed at how well the young children endured the sitting-still time. I especially enjoyed hearing their heartfelt hymns, and I admired the simplicity of their service with all the emphasis on the message and prayers, with no adornments or garnishings.

But I likely won't go back. And I'm certain—in the most friendly way—that will be just fine with them.

Though it's not impossible for an "English" person to join the Amish church, there's only one convert in the local community. I'd heard his name for months and after many attempts at trying to find him home I finally caught Jerry Rocke, pronounced ro-kee, one hot August evening when he'd come in from chores.

A storm creeped in from the west as Jerry sat in a wooden rocker near the open window to catch a breeze and talk about the old days, the days when he owned a three-quarter ton Chevy pickup truck. Back in 1957-58, he'd been in high school and an Apostolic Christian living near Eureka. Then one day he read a fascinating story in the school library's National Geographic magazine about the Amish in Pennsylvania.

He can't explain why he found the plain people so interesting, but he was hooked. He learned a neighbor had taken horses to Arthur for horse sales, so Jerry asked to go along. After a few visits he struck up a conversation with an Amish man. "Think I could get hired as a farmhand down here?" he asked.

Soon after, Jerry—19 then—packed his truck, kissed his family good bye and moved in with the Alvin Beachy family near Arthur.

Now, nearly 50 years later, he laughs at those days living as an outsider among the Amish. They were nice enough to him, he recalls, but he learned afterward that some thought he was spying for the government on the Amish conscientious objectors.

But he worked hard on the farm and soaked up their strange customs and traditions. He began to feel comfortable living without electricity and radio and television, and he began to use some of their Pennsylvania Dutch. Then he put words together into sentences, and he asked questions about the spiritual side of their lives. The answers spoke to his heart, and in the fall of 1958 he began earnestly taking religious instruction with other young Amish in the community. He sold

It's estimated that nationwide there are only 50 to 75 Amish converts.

his pickup truck, and in March 1959 an Amish bishop baptized Jerry Rocke. "I've never once regretted it."

Two years later he married an Amish girl, Lena Kaufman, and the couple had seven children. One of their sons, Daniel, is now an Amish bishop. Lena died of cancer in 1996, and Jerry married Catherine Kaufman, his first wife's cousin.

He's no longer a curiosity, but a respected member of the community. But he is a rarity. Unless born into it, the restrictions and lifestyle changes are too severe. Still, some find it appealing. Jerry estimates as many as 100 people—mostly men—have stopped by to ask about converting. Most think they'd like getting around in buggies and farming with horses and eating dinner by the light of a propane lamp. They

"If somebody's coming for the lifestyle, they won't last. Probably." –Amish convert Jerry Rocke

know little about the spiritual side, and for whatever reason they give up. A few have gone as far as being baptized but left a few years later.

"If somebody's coming for the lifestyle, they won't last. Probably," he said. "They have to have a spiritual hunger."

As the storm came through and the sky blackened, Catherine lit the propane lamp hanging from a hook in the ceiling in their living room. The stark white light bounced off their hardwood floors. She looked for some papers in the dining room with a flashlight while Jerry leaned forward to admit that he didn't want to encourage more people to knock on his door to talk about converting. But he softened it with a condition—If they *really* want to be Amish, he said, he'll do what he can to help. But he shook his head: "Few of 'em do."

Modern-built Amish homes have built-in gas lines for light fixtures.

'Pray … that He would bless your labors …'

–from Rules of a Godly Life

*There are estimates of
140 to 160 cabinet and
woodworking shops
in the Arthur–Arcola area.*

Three or four times a month, Amish cabinetmaker LaVern Schlabach, with his jawline beard, suspenders and homemade denim britches, visits the ritzy Chicago suburbs and works shoulder-to-shoulder with the builders and owners of homes that cost $3 million—or more.

LaVern's shop builds the high-end, ultra-expensive custom cabinets, fireplace mantels and other custom wood pieces for customers in the swank neighborhoods of Hinsdale, Oak Brook, Burr Ridge and the North Shore.

His shop, called Das Holz Haus, which is the Amish Dutch for The Wood House, is tucked away on the northeast side of the rural Arthur community. Its large showroom features incredible "high-end" kitchen displays, paneling and beams, massive cherry fireplace fronts, furniture and even rustic furniture for vacation retreats or log homes.

His trips up north are for more than providing kitchen cabinets.

"We call it a project," LaVern explained. "We not only do the kitchen, we do the butler's pantry, the breakfast area, the study, the laundry room, the mud room, all the bathrooms, and then we go downstairs and we do built-ins around the fireplace and fireplace mantels and all that. It's not just kitchens."

He does the design and the pieces are built in the shop, where he employs about 30. Since the Amish are taught not to value wealth or material possessions, he admits feeling good when he leaves such elaborate homes, many with 7,000 or more square feet, and gets back to his own community. He doesn't envy their wealthy lifestyles.

"I'm just glad to let them have it," he said. "But when we do a project up there, there's a lot of families (down here) fed out of that house. And we buy from a lot of other (Amish) shops in the area. So there are a lot of families fed out of each project."

When he started the business he wanted to provide for his family and give his children a trade they could inherit. He never wanted to get rich, and he doesn't look at his year-end figures to see if he can make more money next year.

"I don't like the idea of getting focused on money," he said. "I think customers (know that) when I walk into a job. When they hand me a blueprint for a $2- or $3-million home, I'm excited about getting to do the work. It's not about the money. It's always about how much more work I can bring home and how it can keep the shop busy and my employees busy."

"When I was a kid, most of the people were on the farm and us children didn't have a lot of contact with non-Amish people. With all the businesses ... there's a lot more now." –Willard Helmuth

Like all Amish businessmen, he oversees the productive enterprise with an eighth-grade education and the help of an Amish tax accountant. He sits at a drafting table and works on projects the old-fashioned way—with a pencil. And he thinks the success or failure of a business can be laid to a couple of basic business principles.

"We need to be good on service, good on delivery, good on time frames, deliver a quality product and believe in customer satisfaction," LaVern said. "The customer's always right, no matter if he's right *or* wrong."

He gives credit to his parents for the success of Das Holz Haus. "When I grew up my parents taught us to work hard—and honesty is the main thing they taught us."

The hum of activity in the Amish shops, estimated at 140 to 160, adds tens

"In our community we have zero unemployment, and we need more help."
—Freeman Beachy

Even if they no longer make their livings from farming, Amish live in the country on small parcels for horses, gardens and hay.

of millions of dollars to the local economy, according to Brian Moody, executive director of Tuscola Economic Development, Inc.

Overall sales from the Amish area totaled more than $100 million in 2006, Moody estimates.

Today, the vast majority of men in the Arthur-Arcola community make their living in woodworking shops or Amish-owned factories or in the construction trades. One can't drive through a new subdivision anywhere in the area without seeing Amish craftsmen—identifiable in their straw hats, dark suspenders and homemade denim breeches—roofing or framing a house.

"The Amish contribute a lot to our local economy," said Theresa Binion, director of the Arthur Visitors center. "A lot of non-Amish people have found employment working for the Amish."

In the 2003 Amish directory, 116 men (born after 1940) listed their occupation as farmer. That's 116 out of 681 households in the directory.

The rest of the occupations listed include woodworker (138), carpenter (35), construction (45), factory (59), shops (170), food (17), masonry (7), and other miscellaneous trades such as farriers, teachers, seamstresses and office workers (28), and the retired (37).

Donald Kraybill, a nationally recognized expert on the Amish and professor of sociology at Elizabethtown College in Pennsylvania, said he thinks the number 116 for farmers might be inflated, meaning those whose primary income comes from farming is much lower.

"I know that in some of the (Arthur-Arcola) church districts, people told me there weren't any farmers in their district," Kraybill said. "Farming is a minority occupation at this point."

But all Amish still live on farms, even if they're 5 acres with a small barn, hayfield and a few cows. Rural living is central to the Amish way of life because it keeps them separate from the world and provides self-sufficiency with large gardens and pasture for horses and a few livestock.

But the price of farm ground—$5,000 to $6,000 an acre—makes it impossible for young families to buy enough land to make a living from it. Many men found a better market for their skills building furniture.

Some, like Freeman Beachy, who is one of the first successful cabinet shop owners, learned how to build and run a business at the same time he kept his faith and principles a priority. When Freeman grew up in the '40s and '50s, he played in his father's small woodworking shop, making wooden whirligigs and lawn ornaments. As a teen he farmed for an uncle and then worked for Walter Schrock, an Amish man who built cabinets in his spare time.

Freeman learned the trade from Walter and decided he liked playing with wood rather than dirt. So after that shop closed, Freeman began building special-order cabinets on his own, and by the late 1970s customers from hundreds of miles drove to F & B Woodworking south of Arthur to buy cabinets and wood-crafted furniture.

Freeman grew the business by listening and following his instincts. He turned out a quality product. And he kept his faith at the forefront.

"I think if we have honesty—if we treat our employees right and our customers fairly, then I feel the good Lord blesses us in ways we can't visualize," Freeman said.

The demand for Amish-built cabinets rapidly grew, but he didn't try to capture all the business and profits. He helped young men open sub-shops and sent them work. He helped create a three-member board that helps couples get their finances out of peril of bankruptcy. Using a pool of money from older Amish couples, the ABC group pays the investors a little more in interest than the local banks and makes mortgages to couples for a little more yet. A similar group offers start-up loans to Amish businesses.

Freeman sold out when health problems slowed him, and he and his wife Bertha volunteer at the Amish-run residential mental health facility near Goshen, Ind., travel by Amtrak and winter in Florida. But when young men seek him out, he gladly gives them advice.

Learn all they can working for someone else. Be sure the product is top quality. And keep their faith the top priority.

"I always tried to say to the Lord when I left the house—'Here I am, Lord. Use me today where you need me.'"

Another early "pioneer" in the cabinet and woodworking shops is Willard Helmuth, who at 55 owns a woodworking business that is so diverse he has more than an acre under roof northwest of Arthur.

He calls it Wilsons Kitchens and More LLC—the "Wil" stands for Willard and the last half for his sons. Its two-story showroom features Amish-made red oak and quartersawn white oak, cherry and maple dining tables and chairs, bedroom suites, and kitchen cabinets and bath vanities.

Many young workers turn over their paychecks to their parents, who save it. When the child marries, the parents help their child with a down payment on a house or a business.

It's touted as the largest Amish-owned furniture store in Illinois, according to the tourist center. Buses often stop to browse and watch the cabinets being made. And though it's all done with power tools, not a kilowatt of electricity from Ameren is delivered to the shop. All the sanders and power saws and routers are run with diesel engines, air compressors and generators. The showroom is lighted by a large skylight and propane lamps.

Why don't the shops advertise that they're Amish? "Well, why would you want to go out and advertise your religion in a product that you make? Really, we don't think it fits."
—Freeman Beachy

Before he opened Wilsons, Willard worked construction and built houses in the area. Willard is also an Amish minister, having been chosen by lot and ordained in 1988. So in addition to running the business, he spends considerable time studying Scripture and preparing for Sundays.

The Amish are taught not to pursue wealth or material possessions, so Willard said he doesn't think of success as being able to give him a better life. To him, success is being able to give his sons and sons-in-law jobs for now and the future.

He tells young Amish businessmen that they won't stay in business if they have a lot of unhappy customers. And he also says: "Don't have your number one priority be on things that rust and rot and don't mean anything anyhow."

"You've got to have an interest in business," he said. "But some things are more important. Family's more important. Family's the top priority."

Freeman Beachy, Willard Helmuth and the other cabinet shop owners didn't realize it at the time, but they've created a niche market for high-end furniture. Today, Amish-made furniture is some of the only wood furniture still made in the United States.

Most wood furniture is made out of the United States, according to Steve Walker, a furniture industry expert with North Carolina State University at Raleigh. Ethan Allen makes about half of its own wood furniture. Thomasville makes none. Companies are outsourcing to China and other Asian markets with lower labor costs.

"Manufacturing (of furniture) in North Carolina and other areas has been absolutely clobbered over the last seven or eight years," Walker said. "We've lost 40,000 jobs in furniture manufacturing. Upholstered furniture is still made here, but wood furniture is where the overwhelming majority of job losses has occurred."

The furniture shops in the Arthur-Arcola area produce pieces that are shipped all over the country by a central wholesale distributor west of Arcola. J & M Representatives has 95 Amish shops that build furniture for them and of those, 45 are in the Arthur-Arcola area. The remainder are in Amish communities in Indiana and Ohio.

They supply 180 different stores around the country selling the furniture under the brand name Simply Amish.

It's high-end furniture made for consumers who are willing to pay for what they perceive as quality, handcrafted pieces of furniture that are beautiful enough and sturdy enough to pass down through the generations as family heirlooms.

"A lot of people have liked the Amish furniture because of the quality, and now we've got a lot more styles," said Butch Mast, one of four partners in J & M. "There's still some that sell the (traditional honey-colored) oak, but it's just not red oak. We have quartersawn white oak and soft maple and hard maple and cherry and walnut and also hickory. And then we have a lot more stain colors. For a lot of years, some manufacturers had only three stain colors, and now we have all the different wood species plus the stains, so we have over 80 different colors available."

"I can honestly say that's never been my goal—to see how much money I could make." –LaVern Schlabach

The Amish furniture can be ordered for custom jobs, too—something the Chinese imports can't accommodate.

"Ours are the heirloom pieces passed down to younger generations—not the veneers that end up in the landfills," Mast said. "And people will pay the prices." J & M employs 37 in the 120,000-square-foot warehouse and has a truck fleet that runs deliveries to the East and West coasts each week. Some of the Simply Amish stores are in Atlanta, Indianapolis and Chicago area. One has opened in downtown Champaign.

One of their largest shipments goes to a Las Vegas store, which is a hot housing market. The Simply Amish furniture is sold in stores in Alaska and Canada.

The Amish-made furniture has created a niche in an otherwise slippery market. Customers will seek it out because it is Amish-made—carrying the perceptual stamp of quality. Kraybill said it's a well-deserved reputation. "Their craftsman-ship is outstanding," he said. "The furniture is very solid."

With J & M Representatives handling distribution of the locally made furniture, the local shop owners can concentrate on production instead of staffing show-rooms or dealing with customers.

As for the cabinet shops—estimated to number about 20 in the Arthur-Arcola area—most have their own contracts with kitchen dealers, especially in the Chicago area. Overhead costs for manufacturing are low because the employees don't need health or retirement benefits.

But the Amish labor is not cheap. The average wage for a woodworker is esti-mated at $16 an hour; starting wages at $10 to $12 an hour. Foremen in some shops might make $50,000 to $60,000 a year.

And there are more jobs than Amish workers to fill them.

The Amish community can boast zero unemployment, and in fact, some shop owners have hired Mexican workers from the Arcola area.

"The Amish import jobs because they have so much job demand," said Brian Moody of Tuscola Economic Development, Inc. "You can look at the census data in 1990 and 2000 and see the manufacturing growth in Douglas County, and the Amish are a major part of that growth. Some of the growth of those businesses has been incredible."

Jim Jurgens, president of the State Bank of Arthur, said it's no exaggeration to say the Amish economy is healthy.

"It's a very vibrant economy," Jurgens said. "They're very industrious and hard-working. There are some very smart (Amish) people out there running busi-nesses. Don't get taken in by the eighth-grade education stuff."

There are showrooms with Amish-made furniture and cabinets throughout the Moultrie-Douglas counties and surrounding area.

Country Charm's showroom on Springfield Road in Arcola draws Interstate traffic, and customers from Chicago, St. Louis and Indianapolis.

"We've had people as far as Colorado who've seen us on the Internet," said manager Vickie Gullion. "Right now we're delivering to Las Vegas."

The big sellers at Country Charm are the bedroom and dining room sets. The standard in the Amish-made furniture—golden medium oak—has been joined by cherry and walnut and the maples, and many different stain colors and styles.

"It's furniture that lasts a lifetime," she said. "It'll pass down to the next genera-tion it's so well made."

One can't drive by Tuscola on I-57 without seeing a barn with AMISHLAND across its roof. Located near the Tanger Outlet mall, the Red Barn offers a buffet,

Amish-owned businesses allow flexible schedules so their employees can attend community events, like weddings, funerals and school activities.

"When a couple marries, we preach they're on their own. They need to be together as a family unit and it's not for (their parents) to be tapping on the children, trying to straighten them out. If they ask for advice, fine. But God said to cleave unto one another, and they can't do that if mom and dad are running the show." —Bishop

*"We have rural roots. We've never been urban people.
It's a little bit like the saying 'You can take the girl
out of the country, but you can't take the country
out of the girl.' If we have space, we like to see
something grow. To me, to watch things grow is to
acknowledge the God of the universe. All these things
didn't just happen. They didn't evolve out of nothing.
The universe runs perfectly, and I'm convinced it
didn't just happen. There's a divine creator behind
it. I believe that, and I believe it with all my heart."*
—David D. Schrock

"There are some (out-of-state Amish) that wouldn't fellowship with us because we're too modern!" –Bishop

"Most of the children will work for the benefit of the family until they're 21 years of age. 'Til then they'll have their clothes furnished, they'll have a buggy and horse furnished and fed, and their medical cares will be taken care of. Everything's furnished for them, too. There are a few families that will give them their age at 18 or 19, but most of us still consider 21 the age when it's proper to do that." –Minister

"The couple goes together and invites all the guests (to the wedding). They take the horse and buggy and drive to all the people's homes and invite them personally. It takes a couple days sometimes." –Minister

"On the Sabbath Day take special note of the wonderful works of God—the creation and governing of the earth and the work of redemption." –from Rules of a Godly Life

"(Amish women) work hard. You'll see them out mowing the yard, working in their big gardens and they put all that stuff up, and they have the kids to take care of too. I know there are English families with big gardens but they also have electricity and air conditioning, so it's a little easier." –Theresa Binion, director of Arthur Visitors Center

"We play softball. Or we like to fly stunt kites. Or we rollerblade. In the winter we skate. In the summer we swim—we've got a pond back here. And we go fishing. We've caught a 2-footer and a 23-inch catfish." –Marcus Graber, 13

"There should be no greater priority than to help our children get to heaven." –from the minutes of the 2006 marriage meeting

bakery, antique and crafts shops, and in the front is a showroom for Amish-made furniture. Amish Country Heirlooms LLC sells furniture made by local craftsmen as well as Indiana and Ohio Amish communities.

Owners Karen and Steven Gingerich bought the showroom from Four Acres, a woodworking-cabinet shop northeast of Arthur. "We learned of the opportunity, and this is where God led us," Karen said. They deliver furniture all around the state; tourists have it shipped.

"A lot of them walk in and say, 'Wow! This stuff is absolutely gorgeous and it's very well made,'" Karen said.

Years ago, the local Amish might have resented AMISHLAND on the roof calling to tourists, but Karen believes they've accepted tourism because it feeds so many Amish families. "I don't know of anybody who has any problems with (tourism)."

And the word "Amish" has become synonymous with quality—though the Amish never advertise their goods as Amish themselves.

"They keep up with the trends and technology and try to bring in new lines of furniture and build what the people are wanting," she said.

Other Amish furniture is sold in shops in Arthur, Tuscola, Atwood and Sullivan, to name a few.

The success of so many Amish businesses makes some wonder if the Amish people have a knack or sixth sense for business.

"Fewer than 5 percent of Amish businesses fail in the first five years," Kraybill said. "Nationally, the rate (among non-Amish) is over 65 percent."

Part of that is due to the support new entrepreneurs receive in the community from experienced businessmen, he said. A business that's foundering can be taken over by three Amish businessmen who will work with the owner to get the problems turned around.

"They really don't have any other choice but to set up businesses," Kraybill said. "Farming isn't an option anymore, and if they want to do something other than working in an English (non-Amish) factory, they have to set up businesses. And since farming is about entrepreneurship, they've transferred those skills of entrepreneurship into business.

"And secondly, growing up on the farm with their religious background and a very strong and deep work ethic, that transfers into business very well.

"They emphasize simplicity—you don't see a lot of overhead in Amish shops. There's no air conditioners, no red carpets. They're very parsimonious."

The Amish won't say it, but some outsiders think this new economy has created a few Amish millionaires.

Amish children do not attend high school, but parents expect a teen to learn a trade, become responsible and acquire work ethic.

Of course Amish are taught not to aspire to wealth, not to be showy or try to outdo their neighbors, so those who are very wealthy are not acting like it. There are no Amish mansions on grandiose estates.

But a comment heard within the community is: "There's too much money."

It's a concern raised most often by the older residents about some of the large, new homes being built by Amish families that are much larger than the simple, practical farmhouses the older generations put up. They see young children drinking cans of soda pop and eating candy bars. They see some Amish homemakers buying some of their clothes ready-made in a few Amish shops.

"In some of the church districts people told me there weren't any farmers in their district, meaning farming was not the source of their primary income." –Donald Kraybill

They see more and more Amish families eating out in restaurants. And there is a lot of traveling these days among Amish families who can afford the treks across country on Amtrak or buses. It's rare, but even a few young people have sailed on the Queen Mary 2 to Europe.

One of the most troubling consequences is that the older teens who have not joined the church have been able to afford pickup trucks or cars.

Kraybill said he sees a love-hate relationship in the community with the shops because of the higher incomes.

"I think they understand it is risky," he said. "It can lead to people buying things they don't need, it can lead to greater consumerism and to pleasure and amusement activities not permitted in the church. If young people have cash in their pockets it's hard to maintain the traditional patterns of frugality and simplicity.

"I think they worry about it," Kraybill said. "It remains to be seen whether it will bring changes that they consider detrimental. I think they know it's risky. But I don't think they know what to do about it."

It's not the first time. Some 20 years ago, similar concerns were raised as the Amish economy shifted from family farms to shops. A common saying was that

A survey of tourists in Lancaster, Pa., found that 88 percent perceive Amish-made products to be of higher quality than other products.

–From the book Amish Enterprise, From Plows to Profits

the lunch pail could end up being the demise of the Amish way of life.

But lots of Amish men pack their lunches these days, catch rides with drivers and go to Charleston, Mattoon, Decatur and Champaign-Urbana for jobs. They make friends with non-Amish and are exposed to a lot more "worldly" ideas and happenings than their parents and grandparents were. Tourists drive through their community with money in their pockets, eager to buy goods made by Amish women and men, believing they're getting quality and good craftsmanship.

One Amish man said he used to put a sign up in his yard that said potatoes for sale, and lots of people pulled in his lane. Some came to buy potatoes, but plenty more pulled in just because they wanted to talk to an Amishman.

But the socializing and exposure to more non-Amish doesn't seem to be hurting them, yet.

By most estimates, 85 to 90 percent of their teenagers decide to become members of the Old Order Faith. And the church leaders are careful to keep the lines drawn—not easing restrictions or regulations.

But another concern expressed frequently in the Amish community is that maybe life is too good. The

"The (Amish) shops are places where the Amish people can be employed within an ethnic context and not exposed to some of the detrimental things they'd be exposed to in English-owned businesses" –Donald Kraybill

Amish were persecuted for generations and then struggled to exist with large families on hard-working farms. Their lives are easier now working in the shops and factories.

"I think easy money is causing us to not need each other quite as much as when we had hardships," said Freeman Beachy. "I think life is too easy. Income is so easy. I actually feel we need hardship—we need hardships to keep drawing us together. And probably other people my age—50 years ago—felt the same way. But usually we don't get serious and need each other until it hurts. And as long as there's plenty of money and plenty of material things available to us, I think we just kind of drift out and away."

One of the Amish bishops agreed. "Hardships keep us on our toes," he said. "We have it pretty easy right now. But that's when we trip."

Starting salaries in the Amish-owned furniture and cabinet shops are about $10 to $12 an hour.

'But without God's blessings … all the labor will be in vain'

—from Rules of a Godly Life

Auctions are a popular pastime in the Amish community. The draft horse and buggy horse auctions draw huge crowds.

Just east of Arthur on 133 and a mile south is the produce auction where wholesale grocers come to bid on Amish-grown vegetables, fruit and greenhouse plants.

Farther east is Beachy's grocery store with its fresh-baked pies, angel food cakes, bulk spices and rolls of sweet butter alongside rows of canned goods and necessities, like propane lamp mantles and blueing for laundry. A horse and buggy waits at the hitching post, but the rest of the parking lot is filled with cars and vans and SUVs. A tour bus from Louisiana stopped earlier that morning.

Down Springfield Road toward Arcola is the Country Salvage Store, again stocked with the groceries and produce that Amish housewives run to for a quick can of Crisco or mushroom soup.

The bright new store straight south of Arthur, the Family Health Foods store, also has big assortments of health supplements and vitamins along with its groceries and baked goods.

South a bit on the County Line Road on the outskirts of Arthur is a shoe shop for good quality boots, a place that sells outdoor lawn furniture and a hardware store with freezer storage, while just up the road is the shop that sells wood-pellet heat stoves and gazebos, and over there is a business that installs vinyl fencing.

Need new cabinets? A bathroom vanity? This big factory here builds trusses and this one builds wood pallets that are delivered all over the U.S., while this guy does masonry and the guy over there builds barns, and just a quarter-mile over there is an upholstery shop.

Near the railroad tracks are the folks who make awnings for campers, and down that way is the woman who serves meals in her home.

Hey! How 'bout a whoopie pie?

This snapshot of the bustling community in the Arthur-Arcola area doesn't begin to capture the diversity of enterprise that goes on at the end of nearly each and every gravel drive that leads to an Amish home.

Scattered among some of the most productive, fertile farmland in the world, the Amish farms are still producing the soybeans and corn for the markets and alfalfa to feed their cows

"After doing this for six years, you can walk into a patch and the plants will talk to you."
–Cephas Yoder, produce farmer

and horses, but a newer economy is booming. It's this economy that the Amish families depend on to feed and clothe their children. It's these cottage industries of the small cabinet and woodworking shops, the tradesmen who hire drivers to take them out into the world to do construction and pour concrete and put up barns, and the factories, like the large truss and pallet-building enterprises. There are greenhouses and produce farmers, salvage grocery stores, bakeries and all kinds of craftsmen and talented ladies. The Shady Crest Orchard and Farmer's Market is a popular tourist stop in the fall with bushel baskets of apples, mums and other fall plants, and an annual tradition of pressing apples into cider.

Cider aficionados can bring their own apples or purchase gallon jugs of cider already made from apples grown at the Shady Crest Orchard.

Cephas Yoder and his wife, Dena, and his sister, Ada Yoder, who jointly operate Shady Crest, begin the apple-pressing operation shortly after Labor Day. It runs through the apple season, ending in late October.

The orchard offers the custom cider pressing only on Thursdays from 7:30 a.m. to 3:30 p.m.

"We had a line of people here this morning, waiting," said Cephas Yoder, 28.

"The best mix (for cider) is Red Delicious, Yellow Delicious and Jonathan."
–Cephas Yoder

Levi Beachy started his business with 25 chickens, selling eggs from his front porch.

"One year we had as many as 20 people lined up, and one man came as early as 4 a.m. to get a first turn."

Most of his customers bring their own plastic jugs to save a quarter. Cephas said he's known customers who drive for an hour-and-a-half for the cider. The farm's fall offerings also include homegrown mums and asters, pumpkins, squash and, of course, several varieties of apples.

The Yoders use hydraulic motors to run some of the equipment, rather than electricity. The apples are run through a machine that gives them a wash, and then they are chopped before being put into the press, which extrudes the cider with 1,800 pounds per square inch of pressure.

"We can do a 20-gallon batch in 20 to 25 minutes," Cephas said. The cider is bottled and capped in sterile plastic jugs and kept cool.

The Shady Crest Orchard was started nearly 30 years ago by Martha and Lonnie Yoder, the parents of Cephas and Ada. Lonnie Yoder began offering the custom cider pressing, and the orchard remains one of a very few in the area that provides the service. The orchard has about five acres devoted to apple production. In August 2007, the Yoders moved the operation down their long lane to a new large barn that sits alongside the road, still on the County Line Road, with more room for produce and parking for visitors.

Fridays and Saturdays are pie days at Beachy's Grocery Store on county road 200E, southeast of Arthur. Pie day means that the hot apple, cherry, pumpkin and berry pies are brought out and set on top of grocery carts to cool while coveys of non-Amish men and women hover around to snag a few.

More than 100 little 6-inch pies are put out and about 70 of the steaming-hot 9-inch pies. With selling prices of $3.50 and $6.99, folks consider them a bargain, and they often load up on fresh-baked breads and angel food cakes, whoopie pies, cinnamon rolls, bulk spices and a big assortment of soup starters and puddings, candies, canned goods, rolled butter and other groceries.

"We had a busload from Louisiana on the way up to Holland, Mich., stop in," said Levi Beachy. He started the business by selling eggs on his front porch in

1980. The egg business continued to grow, and when he began adding groceries and fresh baked goods, the business expanded into four different buildings.

Most of the customers are non-Amish, strangely enough. Levi at 68, with white hair and beard, is stepping out of the business. He sold it to his son, Melvin.

"He's a third of the boys and a fifth of the family," Beachy said. "He lives here and does the farming. He milks around 70 cows and has about 600 head of hogs, and farms."

"My father used to say he only liked two kinds of pie—hot and cold."
–Annie Ellen Otto

Beachy had to meet state requirements in order to make and sell baked goods there, so he hired rides into Parkland College in Champaign for a week. "I passed the test and now I'm certified," he said.

Diesel generators run the freezers and coolers, and occasionally on very hot days, air conditioning. The store is lit with skylights and propane lamps, and the store cannot accept credit cards because there is no phone line to verify. And, like all Amish businesses, it is not open on Sundays.

The SUVs, pickups and farm trucks park on the north side. On the south side are Amish buggies, carts and horses, swishing their tails at pesky flies. In between, in the shade of a large metal pole barn, the two cultures meld into a friendly group of bidders and sellers as the Arthur Produce Auction gets under way.

The auctioneer and staff are Amish, while most of the buyers come from far away to purchase produce for their roadside stands or farmers' markets. Every Tuesday and Friday during the growing season, the sale starts at 10 a.m. in the barn southeast of Arthur. The produce is grown by Amish farmers as well as by growers from the region.

"The quality's always good, and the prices are good, too," said Keith Cooper, who drives 120 miles from Stilesville, Ind. He buys produce to sell in front of his hardware store. "And I just like everybody over here," he said. "I like to come."

One day the pallets were loaded with boxes of cabbages, eggplants, blackberries, bing cherries, sweet corn, summer squash, green beans, blueberries, onions, tomatoes, the prolific zucchini and more. About 70 bidders bought the items in bulk—50 cantaloupes, 30 pounds of tomatoes, 50 pounds of sweet corn. But small lots of produce were also offered at the end of the auction for those who wanted a

The Arthur Produce Auction started with 20-some Amish families in 2004.

couple pounds of tomatoes or a box of cucumbers to pickle. Giant iced cinnamon rolls and other treats, including hot sandwiches, are sold, so it's not surprising that many of the "buyers" admit to being regulars who come for the socializing as much as for good deals on produce.

Amish-made quilts sell for $600 and up. "Considering all the hours put into it, you have to love it to do it. And I do." –Mattie Miller

"See ya Tuesday," Elfrieda Brieschke of Sadorus called to another regular who left with just one melon.

Elfrieda and her husband attend every Tuesday and Friday, largely for the fun of it. The Brieschkes buy items from the small-lots part of the auction, such as six pints of cherries, and they will divvy them up with friends later.

"Oh my, you should see this place right before Mother's Day," Elfrieda said. "The floor is covered, just full of flowers."

Bill Snyder comes up from Charleston. He and his wife can buy enough to can and freeze. "They go cheap sometimes," he said. "Quality's good."

Cephas Yoder of rural Arthur is one of the two Amish auctioneers and one of the local growers who supplies the auction. He'd like to see even more Amish dedicate land to vegetables and fruits to supply the auction. Similar Amish-owned auctions in other communities have become big business, supplying restaurants and wholesalers. The Arthur Produce Auction is only into its third season. About 20 shareholders, mostly Amish, own and operate it. The auctions run from May through October, when the barn is filled with pumpkins, squashes, mums and asters. At the end of the season, the shareholders and other Amish regulars invite all the buyers to join them for a potluck dinner. They set up tables in the auction house, and the Amish women bring in hot casserole dishes while others bring desserts.

"Oh, it's wonderful," said Eberhard Brieschke of the food and the fellowship.

Emma Gingerich, the auction manager, agrees. "It keeps us busy, and the next day is always bookwork. But we meet a lot of nice people."

About 350,000 tourists visit Arthur, Arcola and local tourist attraction Rockome Gardens each year. The Arcola exit on I-57 has a sign encouraging drivers to turn their radios to local 530-AM to hear about the local attractions.

The Amish Interpretive Center in Arcola attracted 18,000 visitors last year. About two buses a week in the spring, summer and fall come to Arthur to see the large museum filled with artifacts donated by Amish families. The center also has a media room for an 18-minute video about the local Amish and a gift shop. The center arranges for tour guides, who hop on the bus tours to Amish farms, homes and for Amish meals. The center is overseen by a board of three local men who were raised Amish but left the church—J.B. Helmuth, Wilmer Otto and Fred Helmuth.

Amish-run events like the Tri-County Horse Sales, held near Arcola in March and September, draw thousands from all over the country. The Horse Progress Shows draw thousands, as well as horse sales like the Heart of America Pony Sale and the East Central Illinois Standardbred and Pony Sale. And monthly, the Arthur Sale Barn on the north side of Arthur has auctions for horses, tacks, livestock and small animals like chickens and goats.

Sources: Susan Foster, the executive director of the Arcola Chamber of Commerce; Amber Kauffman, director of the Amish Interpretive Center; Theresa Binion, director of the Arthur Visitors Center.

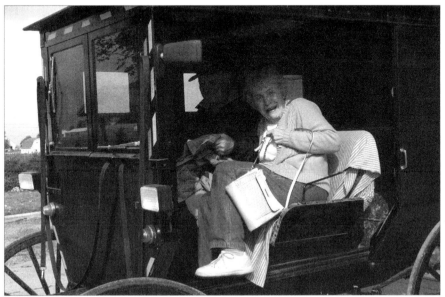

"(Tourists) like to see the differences in the cultures. They like to experience that home-cooked meal and they like to get back to simpler times." –Stella Eads

'Wives are to be ... temperate and trustworthy'

–1 Timothy 3:11

An Amish woman uses about a dozen straight pins to fasten the bodice of her dress and the apron over it.

In the Amish community, single women can work in the shops and factories or teach, but when they marry, most stay home for the more important career of overseeing the household and garden.

And when the married women have children, they do not work outside the home, away from the children. It's one of their unwritten rules: mothers are to keep the house and raise the children. The women plant and tend huge gardens to provide canned vegetables throughout the winter and spring, they freeze fruits and make jellies and jams, they raise and butcher chickens, sew all the clothes for themselves, their husbands and the children, do the laundry using wringer washers and clothes lines, cook the meals, keep the house clean and windows washed, and many also take care of mowing the yards and tilling the gardens.

As the wood and craft shops have cropped up in the community, many Amish women have taken on added responsibilities of helping in their husband's businesses. Some do bookkeeping, or they pitch in and work in the shops, running sanding machines or sweeping up.

And some Amish women have started their own sideline businesses, such as cooking meals in their homes for tourists, upholstery, selling quilts and crafts, selling baked goods and weaving rugs, just to mention a few.

Most people say the Amish families have four to seven children, but there are plenty with nine or more.

Church leaders teach that birth control interferes with God's natural plan for couples, so it is not used unless there are health concerns. Most mothers nurse their babies, and these days, some young mothers enjoy the convenience of disposable diapers, especially for church or other events away from home.

All Amish mothers carry their babies in their arms and do not use heavy-duty plastic baby carriers. During church services the little ones nap on their mother's shoulders or across their laps. There are also no car seats for Amish youngsters in the buggies.

"A Christian mother doesn't have any place to be in a factory or anything like that. She's to be home with her children." –Bishop

Babysitters are rarely used because families usually take their children wherever they go, and if they can't, grandparents or siblings would likely watch the children.

Mothers also take responsibility for teaching their daughters how to cook, bake, can and do other household chores. They teach their daughters how to sew clothes and to do quilting. The oldest girls and boys in the family share responsibilities for caring for the littlest ones, and frequently have a little brother or sister on their hips.

The Amish women who have opened sideline businesses fit their jobs around their home duties. And in their spare time many also are helping with the care of elderly parents and in-laws. The Amish do not put their elderly in nursing homes. Many women also keep time in their schedules to participate in get-togethers, like work days. These are typically a day set aside each month when the women in a family will take turns helping each other out. If one sister is hosting, the others will help her

Sewing is part of an Amish woman's life. Most married women make their own dresses, coats, jackets and sleep gowns and also the denim pants, shirts, jackets and coats for their husbands and children. The paper patterns have changed little through the generations.

with a project of her choice, such as quilting or sewing or cleaning floors or windows. They eat lunch and enjoy the time together visiting. The women also make time for quilting bees, especially when a quilt is being made for a charity auction or to raise money for one of the Amish schools. When a neighbor's sick, an Amish woman will cook up a casserole or pies, and they routinely take food to wakes and funerals.

"It's much like a large family. There are some difficulties, some disagreements ... But we know each other. And when we meet each other, we wave and so on." –David D. Schrock

As more Amish women take on home-based businesses, some new phenomena are popping up. A variety store opened in downtown Arthur that sells Amish clothing for women, men and children, handsewn by Amish seamstresses. The ready-made clothes indicates some of the Amish women are too busy to sew, or perhaps some can afford to not *have* to sew. Also, more Amish families can be seen eating in restaurants. Some conservative Amish are concerned about this subtle change in their culture away from three home-cooked meals a day.

Amish women never wear slacks. On extremely cold days, they may wear sweatpants under their dresses.

Women in the Amish community are becoming entrepreneurs, finding outlets for them to do work they enjoy from their homes, and also bring in some extra income. The following vignettes are of a few of these local women who've taken that step and work from their homes, either part-time or for some long, hard days.

Annie Ellen Otto has a light-up smile that quickly makes strangers feel warm and welcome, and a trace of an accent in her English that points to her native Pennsylvania Dutch.

Annie Ellen and her husband Melvin have a large, white-sided two-story home with a huge, neatly tended garden. She cans and freezes hundreds of quarts of vegetables and fruits, and they butcher beef, pigs and chickens so she's not beholden to grocery stores for a meal.

The couple share their garden with their seven children—now all grown—and see all of them all the time. Two live at home, their oldest son and his wife have built a home on the back of Melvin's and Annie Ellen's property, and the other children live in the Arthur community, too. Annie Ellen keeps a large pantry in the basement, not far from her gas-powered wringer washing machine. Clothes lines stretch across the backyard of their 20-year-old home. A large room on the back of their house can hold the 125 or more for church. Some walls fold away to create one giant room.

Annie Ellen's has had other responsibilities, too. A couple times a month, Annie hitched the horse up to a buggy and traveled south to care for her 96-year-old mother-in-law—a task she willingly undertook. "They took care of us when we were small, and now we want to do that for our parents," she said. And like many Amish homemakers, she's also a partner and worker in the business she and her husband started and run from their home.

Their Otto Canvas Shop makes canvas tops for boats, campers, wagons and other implements. But they started in 1972 with a roll of canvas, a broken sewing machine and an idea, she said, with not a lick of knowledge about how to do it. They learned it all by trial and error. She'd been sewing clothes for herself and her brothers since she was 11, and she'd worked in an upholstery shop as a single woman, so she figured out how to cut and sew the boat covers and then taught Melvin.

As they struggled to get the business on its feet, they also shared the household work and garden and child rearing.

"He was as much a part of the children growing up as I was as a mother," she said. "That's the only way we made it."

She's been able to step out of the day-to-day work in the shop as three of her sons stepped in. She started a part-time business selling Conklin products, a line of health, cleaning, agricultural, automotive and other products, and she also sells vitamin and health supplements. The family has a phone shack out near a shed to take care of their business calls.

For fun, she and Melvin love to see the country, and they've traveled by train from coast to coast. But it's their faith that is at the root of all they do. They pray together and read Bible Scripture every morning. They say silent prayers before and after each meal. And in the evenings they pray or read Scripture. This is the life she chose, she said, and it's the life God wants her to lead. She feels lucky to have been born into an Amish family.

"God is in our surroundings. He's what we live for," she said. "If we have a problem, the first thing we ask is, 'what would God think?'"

Six of her seven children are Amish; the other married and became a Beachy Amish, which is a conservative arm of the Mennonites. Annie Ellen feels fortunate

Amish women do not cut their hair. They wear it parted in the middle and pulled into a bun at the back of their heads. They keep their heads covered with plain scarves, white organdy head "covers" or black-brimmed hats. This is based on Scripture from 1 Corinthians Chapter 11, including this verse: "But if a woman have long hair, it is a glory to her, for her hair is given her for a covering."

Amish women wear no makeup, perfume or jewelry, including wedding rings and watches. Their purses are black and plain.

"Everybody goes to church; everybody takes their children to church. All the children attend church." –Minister

to have her children nearby and involved in church. On Christmas Eve, their children and families come home and stay overnight. There's a lot of laughing and cooking and fun. They swap a few gifts.

"And we do a lot of singing," she said. "Singing always goes with Christmas—and prayer."

———

Oba and Lorene Herschberger, who live at the far south edge of the settlement near Sullivan, raised 13 children born within a span of 17 years. Oba came from a family of 14; Lorene from a family of 19.

Raising such a large family didn't overwhelm them. "We didn't think about it," Oba said. "We had what they call a big buggy—a three-seater—and when the oldest boys were old enough they followed behind in their buggies, and that's the way we went to church and that's the way we went everywhere. We didn't think about it. The oldest ones helped take care of the youngest ones, and we had a lot of chores and everybody knew what to do. If you had 13 in one year it would be a catastrophe, but actually we were more organized when the kids were home than we are now."

The Herschbergers had six bedrooms and two bathrooms in their farmhouse; now three children live at home and all but one of their children live locally. They have 29 grandchildren.

When Oba's father, Chris E. Herschberger, died he left 664 direct descendants. "For here it was a record," he said. "We heard one other person might've had more (in the U.S.)."

———

Amish women wear dark stockings or anklet socks and dark tie-up shoes, usually dark sneakers. If it is hot, they go barefoot. A very few have begun to wear sandals, but this is stirring controversy with some of the older members of the church.

One day, Betty Graber had done her laundry on her wringer-washing machine at 5 a.m., hung the clothes on the line to dry, fed five of her children and husband breakfast, had daily devotions with the family, seen them off to work and school, and then walked across the large gravel lane to her two large greenhouses.

A thin, attractive woman of 41, she's a self-educated horticulturist, having learned all the ins-and-outs of growing perennials, annuals and herbs through reading books and attending workshops. She's learned to market the greenhouse with advertising and posters, and build a roster of reliable return customers. Her business keeps her busy from the start of January, ordering the seed and pots and fertilizers and all, through the end of June.

In her business, she oversees the ordering, planting and growing. Ben, her husband, works as a carpenter and helps her with maintenance and other chores and tasks when needed, but the greenhouse is primarily her responsibility.

Betty said when the business begins to slow at the end of June she spends the next six months recharging. That's when she'll do the sewing for her family, and she'll visit her mother and sisters more. "Those are things I know I can't do during the greenhouse season."

She gets great satisfaction from the greenhouse and hearing the comments of her customers. "I want to do all I can so they have a good plant all summer long," Betty said. "And then when they come back next year, I want them to tell me how those plants did."

She gets her children involved working in the greenhouse when she can. Sometimes she'll take plants to sell at the Arthur Produce Auction and buy fresh produce for her children to sell at the greenhouse. Her sons have also dug up worms to sell to customers. Tourists will ask questions about her way of life, and some have asked her why she wants to be Amish. She's learned to be honest. "I tell them that this is what I want to be," Betty said. "For me, this is my way of life. It's my choice."

Working at home allows her to contribute to the family income. But it also keeps her grounded and on their farm. "And we have more time at home with our family," she said.

Her name is Mattie, and most days she can be found sitting at her Singer treadle sewing machine, lit by the soft light from an east window, sewing and cutting from early morning until dark.

Mattie Miller knows the patterns and puzzles of quilts like the names of the family and old friends she's acquired in her 75 years.

She's lived all of them in the Arthur community, and still lives on the farm she moved to in the 1950s as a young bride. Her stepmother gave her three handmade quilts to start housekeeping with—one a flower garden, and another a flower basket, which Mattie still has.

Growing up one of 19 children, Mattie started sewing when she was about 12. She can't count how many quilts she's pieced in her lifetime. Hundreds, she says.

A Mattie Miller quilt costs $450 to $600. She's sold them to people all over the country; more than 100 Broken Star pattern quilts went to a woman from Clinton.

Amish women consider their husbands the leaders in their partnership. A couple will talk over issues, but the husband makes the decision and she is to respect it.

Amish women cook their big meal of the day at noon. A summer noon meal might include a piece of canned beef with gravy, mashed potatoes, corn on the cob, sliced tomatoes and onions, cole slaw, homemade bread and apple butter, and a scratch cake or cobbler. A summer supper might be homemade bologna served on one slice of bread, sliced tomatoes and onions, and a dessert. Cold soups are also popular suppers in the summers; hot soups in the winter.

"I think it was made in 1950. You have to oil it and change needles and that's about it. Once in a while it'll have to go to the shop." –Mattie Miller

For a summertime family treat, an Amish wife and mother might pop up a kettle of popcorn. The whole family, including grandma and grandpa in the daudy house next door, will sit outside in the shade to share the snack, the fine weather and the company.

The income helps fuel the passion she has for piecing the patterns with names like Wedding Ring, Texas Lone Star and Log Cabin. Her husband, Henry, a woodworker and Amish bishop, died three years ago, but at one time he helped cut the fabric for her.

"Cutting's the hardest part," she said.

The Amish quilts made to sell feature vibrant prints and calicos, but the quilts the Amish women make for themselves are pieced with solid colors only. Some Amish quilts have embroidered blocks with family members' names and birth dates, or birds, flowers and butterflies. Practical and thrifty, an Amish woman makes a quilt to fulfill a need, not a decorating scheme. And they use it until it's worn out. The one on her bed is plain and worn. Mattie lives in the white daudy house, or grandpa house, next to her son Ernest and his family. Her health is good, but her knees are bad.

"The doctor said he thought I wore 'em out peddling the machine." She laughed.

Ruth Yoder is one of about half-a-dozen Amish women who serves meals in her home to tourists.

She lives up a long lane, far south of Arthur, near Sullivan with her husband Reuben. Ruth met us at the door in her white head covering and dark burgundy-colored polyester dress. We sat around the kitchen table capable of seating 10. She started serving meals eight years ago because she wanted to help with the living and didn't want to work outside the home. Reuben farms some land, installs and finishes wood floors, and they raise and sell Belgian draft horses. Plus, it gives her the freedom to babysit grandchildren when needed and also to travel to visit a daughter in Virginia. She has no problem inviting strangers into her home. "I'll answer any question about the way we live," she said. "But I don't like to take questions about religion. I don't feel like I can explain it that well."

She has fed up to 50. In addition to 10 in her kitchen, she can seat 10 in her south room, 10 in her front room and 15 in the living room.

She serves fried chicken, salisbury steak, dressing, mashed potatoes and gravy, salad with her own sweet onion dressing, bread, rolls and a vegetable—usually green beans. For dessert she offers a choice of a fruit pie and a cream pie. Many of her guests are local church groups who visit from neighboring towns. Having 50 for dinner is not a big deal for her, she said. She cooked for the weddings of her three daughters and some of those meals were for 300 to 400 guests.

Ruth also sells her own peanut butter spread and sweet onion dressing. She has both bottled for her commercially to meet state health and safety standards, and they are sold at Amish shops. The sweet onion dressing is on the salad bar at Yoder's Kitchen in Arthur. The peanut butter spread is a mixture of peanut butter, marshmallow cream and light Karo syrup, traditionally served in the light meal after church on Sundays. Ruth advertises her meals through the local weekly papers.

When Doris Yoder grew up the oldest in her family of eight, she learned to cook at an early age. By the age of 10, she'd baked her first cake.

And now, she's one of several women in the Amish community near Arthur who supplement the family income by baking and cooking for others.

Yoder, 48, has published two cookbooks, "A Matter of Taste" and "A Matter of Taste Volume 2." From her two-story farm home on the western side of the Amish community, she also serves meals to crowds or even just a few.

She does baking on order, mostly breads and her specialty—cinnamon rolls—and makes gift baskets of home-baked goods and candies and other small gifts.

She also caters weddings. Because she gets around her community with horse and buggy, she hires drivers to get her and her helpers to the wedding halls to serve

"I think (the Amish), probably like anybody else, get tired of the traffic. But a lot of them realize they need it because there's not enough farmground to go around. They have to do something to supplement the income for their family. And part of that's tourism." –Theresa Binion, director of the Arthur Visitors Center

the meals. One wedding she did last summer in Mahomet served 225 to 250 and offered roast beef and chicken, cheese potatoes, broccoli-cauliflower salad, hot rolls and also cheese trays and fruit trays.

"Doris is an excellent cook," said Theresa Binion, director of the Arthur Tourist Center. "I know that—personally I know that."

Binion said she and her husband have taken friends to Yoder's for meals, and the food received rave reviews.

"She's just really good. The things that she fixes!" Binion said.

Yoder and her husband, Gerald, who runs a printing business, have been mar-

Many Amish homemakers have two stoves and two refrigerators because they often cook for large crowds of family and neighbors. The spares are often in the basement.

Amish women use organdy to make their white head covers. They use starch to make them hold their shape, and form the hats around rolls of toilet paper.

Amish women use the heavy flatirons that are heated with little propane tanks.

They are expensive, sometimes as much as $100, and are used most often to make their white head covers and black bonnets.

They use polyester blends to make most of their clothes so ironing isn't needed.

ried almost 20 years. Before marrying, she did cooking and housecleaning for "English" (non-Amish) families and worked as head cook at Arthur's now-closed Dutch Oven restaurant and at the restaurant in Chesterville that has gone through a few different owners and name changes.

"Everything just kind of went from one to another, but it was always cooking," she said. "And I do like to cook."

The recipes in her cookbooks are ones she uses herself or has acquired from her mother or others in the community. She's also compiling a new cookbook from the aged, faded pages of a recipe collection that belonged to her mother's mother. She hopes to have it done for family members for a reunion next summer.

The largest meal Yoder has served in her home was to a crowd of 78. Typically they are groups of 25 to 40, sometimes church groups from the area.

She said a typical dinner at her house for 25 would include fried chicken, roast beef (or ham loaf), mashed potatoes and gravy, noodles or dressing, green beans, a lettuce salad and homemade breads and rolls. Dessert would be four pies, probably two cherry and two coconut cream.

She's made good friends by serving the meals in her home and enjoys meeting new people.

Sometimes, she admits, visitors are surprised by her Amish home. Some expect that they will not have running water or indoor bathrooms.

"And some are amazed at our (propane gas) lights," she said.

Because the Amish take turns holding church in their own homes, they are proficient at moving furniture out of the way and setting up tables and benches to feed a crowd.

Yoder's a tireless worker who rises at 4:30 or 5 a.m. to do her laundry and hang it out to dry before beginning her cooking and baking and other chores. In addition, she also runs the kitchen and grill several long days a month at the Arthur Sale Barn on the north side of town.

Some of the regulars tell her that her cinnamon rolls and tenderloin sandwiches make their trips to Arthur worthwhile, she said.

In the larder

An Amish woman's vegetable garden is typically large, well-tended, weeded and watered. She takes responsibility for it, and she can feed her family throughout the year with the items she cans and freezes. Many take satisfaction in a well-stocked pantry at the end of the summer.

What does an Amish woman do in the summertime? Here's a look at one woman's basement pantry:

Green beans	37 quarts	Apple pie filling	6 quarts
Corn	14 pints	Peaches	56 quarts
Pickles	50 quarts	Pears	2 quarts
Tomatoes	15 quarts	Apricots	3 quarts
Tomato juice	33 quarts	Strawberries	35 quarts
Ketchup	30 pints	Black raspberries	25 quarts
Pizza sauce	45 pints	Cherries	26 quarts
Vegetable soup	7 quarts	Grapes	20 quarts
Canned chicken,		Grape juice	17 quarts
beef & pork	58 quarts	Cider	12 quarts
Applesauce	50 quarts	Apple butter	40 quarts

Frozen foods stored in the locker at Arthur include home-butchered beef, pork and fryers, as well as corn, peas, cole slaw, broccoli and strawberries.

When it's a couple's turn to host church, the wife's mother, sisters and sisters-in-law and women neighbors may spend two or three days helping to clean the house from top to bottom.

Amish couples are discouraged from using birth control, though there can be exceptions for health reasons. A married woman would likely have four to seven children.

Women in a family get together for work days once a month. The mother and her grown daughters and daughters-in-law will take turns meeting at each other's home to help with cleaning, baking, canning, sewing or quilting.

'Blest be the tie that binds'

–from Lizzie Otto's memory book

This book opened with the story of Lizzie Otto's death. This is the story of her life. Not because she achieved any distinction, fame or elevated status in her Amish community near Arthur and Arcola. But precisely because she didn't. Her life's experiences as a wife and mother were not much different from any other devout Amish woman born early in the last century.

Lizzie spent all but three of her 96 years in Illinois, having been born the oldest of eight children to Amish parents who left the chinch bugs and droughts in Kansas behind for the promise of better land near Arthur.

Lizzie grew up attending the one-room country schools. She wrote in her family history that her parents needed extra help with the farm and caring for her younger brothers and sisters, so she stayed home after seventh grade. She never graduated eighth grade, but she said she learned more math by raising and selling broilers and eggs.

She married Rudy Otto on Sept. 28, 1933. Both were 22. They served their 135 to 140 wedding guests fried chicken, a rare treat in those Depression days. The couple's first home was in a tenant's house south of Chesterville, where Rockome Gardens is now. For $5 a week, Rudy and Lizzie milked cows, tended hogs, chickens, horses, cattle and did all the other farm chores. "At the time ... eggs were down to 10-12 cents a dozen. A good milk cow was $25 or less," she wrote in the memory book.

Through the years the couple worked and rented from several farm owners, living in small, often dilapidated houses to raise their family. In 1953, the couple purchased a place northeast of Arthur for their 10—at that time—children. It had two small bedrooms upstairs, a 10-by-12 bedroom downstairs, no basement, and it needed a lot of repairs, including the outbuildings and pastures.

"We had built up a good Guernsey herd of milk cows from calves we raised but ... without fences to keep the cows out of the bush they ate acorns (and) our Guernseys were soon 'down the hill,'" she wrote. "But such is life, full of joys and strife. But with patience and faith we were richly blessed and got more than we really deserved."

Lizzie worked alongside Rudy through the years fixing up their home and farm, as well as doing all the laundering, cooking and baking, and sewing for the family. She made extra money selling chickens and eggs and cream.

They put in a large garden and planted fruit trees. "I washed in an old brooder house," she wrote. "The wash water was heated out in the yard."

Of those hectic, difficult times she said: "We never went to bed hungry or went without a meal. We made do with what we had."

Rudy had experience helping farmers butcher their cattle and hogs, so in 1955 he opened his own butcher shop and did that in addition to farming. One son remembered they stuffed and smoked their own bologna, sometimes 150 pounds at a time, and he hated to help with the chore of cleaning tongues, brains and sweet breads. Rudy closed the shop in 1968, when health department requirements became too expensive to meet.

And by 1978, nine of their children had married and two daughters lived at home. But in the morning of Oct. 4, 1978, Rudy went to the timber behind their home to cut firewood. Two of the older children, working to build a stall behind the barn, noticed they hadn't heard the motor of their father's chain saw for a while. They went to the woods and found him unconscious and severely injured. A big tree had fallen into a smaller tree, and the smaller trunk snapped under the weight, striking Rudy with terrific force in the forehead. An ambulance rushed him to the emergency room in Decatur for surgery but he never regained consciousness and died seven days later. He was just 67. He and Lizzie had celebrated their 45th wedding anniversary a few weeks before. She had a difficult time, losing her partner for so many years, but like she always did she dug in her heels and made do with life as it was.

She stayed on the home place and helped care for her elderly mother, who lived to be 101, and she helped her children with their families, including 46 grandchildren. She pieced quilts for many of her children and grandchildren, kept a large garden that she weeded and preserved, and she welcomed 150 great-grandchildren into the world. Until she was 90, she could name each one of her 46 grandchildren by name and many of her great-grandchildren.

In the family memory book, one of her grandchildren wrote: "Who all remembers the way Grandma would bend you over her knee and pretend to spank you? She also often gave us 'horsey' rides by crossing her legs and sitting us on her foot. We never tired of that and always begged for 'one more.'

"Another thing we never got tired of were the Farmer Brown stories she read to us. If Mom had to go somewhere and Grandma babysat, after dinner she always rocked us to sleep on 'There Are Days I'd Like To Be All Alone,' 'When The Roll Is Called Up Yonder,' and 'We'll Work Til Jesus Comes.'

"If we'd see Grandma come walking up the road, we'd run out the lane to meet her and she always stopped and gave each of us a 'bear' hug and would swing the little ones high."

Lizzie wrote in the memory book that looking back on her life, "I can see I've made many mistakes but hope I can be forgiven."

In the family memory book, when addressing the struggles she and Rudy faced to make a living and raise their large family, she wrote: "Lots of hard work but Scripture does say that we are to 'work with sweat on our brow.' That's what we really did, but it did not hurt us."

And in a postnote following one of her daughter's recollections, Lizzie wrote: "Yes, you older girls always lived in small, cold houses but we were all together and I felt happier than many with nice, warm houses with plenty of room. I once read somewhere it said like this—A mansion without love is only a hut, but a hut with love is a mansion. So I hope we lived in a mansion after all."

Lizzie fell when she was 87 and broke her leg, and though the doctors weren't sure she'd walk again, she did. Her health began to decline gradually after that and at 90 she had her first stroke. But like most Amish families, her children jumped in to help her. And when her health continued to decline, a daughter moved Lizzie into her home near Sullivan. It was there that Lizzie eventually died on Aug. 14, 2007, but it was not without daily visits from children and their spouses, grandchildren, neighbors and nieces and nephews.

A few days before she died she'd suffered another stroke that knocked her into unconsciousness. Lizzie lay with her eyes closed, motionless, except for her left arm, which would thrash around at times.

But one evening, while family had come to visit her, they stepped into the kitchen to eat dinner. A short while later, a daughter-in-law peeked in to check on Lizzie. Lizzie's eyes were wide open, intently gazing at something over her head.

Lizzie's left arm reached as far as she could stretch it as she tried to grasp at something in the air. She kept reaching and gazing and trying to grab at it and finally after several minutes, she closed her eyes and her arm once again rested at her side.

Her children and their spouses gathered around her bed and sang hymns, just as they'd done for their father when he lay dying at Decatur Memorial Hospital from his head wound.

The singing seemed to coax Lizzie into a deeper, relaxed sleep. And she died within a few hours.

There is no doubt, the children believe, that angels came to visit Lizzie that night, and that she saw them clearly and vividly surrounding her bed. She reached out to them to grab hold, to go with them.

The young great-grandchildren are told that she went to heaven. But the Amish believe that Lizzie and all who die who have led good Christian lives are at rest and that they will remain there until the second coming of Christ on Judgment Day.

One of the mementoes her children keep is a coffee cup that she gave to each of them at an Otto family reunion. She selected this prayer to be printed on the cups: "O, Father, Lead us gently by the hand Through sun and shadow of the future land, Dim and untraveled lies the way before, O Father, lead us evermore."

"She's in a restful place," her son Melvin said. "We call it Paradise."

'Lead our beloved youth to … Jesus'

–Amish prayer

I t's shortly after noon on a cold winter day and a group of Amish children are skating on a frozen pond of standing water in a cornfield.

The little girls, ranging in age from maybe 4 to 11, are barelegged in their dresses, wearing black coats and black bonnets. The little boys have dark stocking hats and their homemade dark coats and denim breeches. The girls and boys run from the cornfield onto the ice, sliding as far as they can from the momentum in their tennis shoes and boots. No house is nearby, so they'd hiked a pretty good distance in the cold to get to the pond.

One other day, in the heat of mid-August, a 9-year-old named Wilbur is driving his pony cart around and around the gravel driveway. The freckle-faced boy, whose dark eyes peek out from under a straw hat, is just learning to drive the cart, hitched to a brown pony.

In addition to closed buggies, most Amish families keep small open carts for the children to use to get back and forth to school.

"We direct our children's lives toward being Amish, in the hopes that they will be." –Minister

Amish children accompany their parents most everywhere. The Amish don't use babysitters or daycare centers.

He's pleased he's reached the age that allows him to drive the cart by himself. A few days earlier he'd been able to drive it out into the hayfield to help the men baling hay. He shows how he can back the pony and cart up. Hop in, he says, take a ride.

The Amish children grow up in different environments than other children. Since they have no televisions, they have not been exposed to Sesame Street, cartoons or TV sitcoms. They don't play video games or have tape players, radios or stereos. They don't know Hannah Montana from Scooby Doo and don't go to movies or watch DVDs.

They often come from families of four to seven children, and they are expected to "chore," meaning help take care of the buggy horses, other livestock and whatever else needs taking care of. They all grow up on farms, even if it's only three acres, and in most families they have assigned tasks.

They like to play softball and volleyball, but there are no leagues or sports teams. The Amish love to sing hymns but do not use musical instruments, so the children do not take piano or tuba lessons. They don't take swimming or dance lessons. The Amish children don't participate in theater groups or art clubs.

They do learn to do the laundry and cook. One day, Loretta, a just-turned 12-year-old, had done the entire laundry for her family of nine on the wringer washer, hung it to dry, fixed the noon meal, and taken down the dry laundry, folded it and put it away. Her mother had been occupied canning bucket after bucket of tomatoes.

The boys help in the fields or with washing the buggy or keeping the garden clean of weeds or the yard mowed. The older children do heavier chores—helping cut or rake hay, put hay up in the barn.

The activity level of Amish children intrigued kinesiologists from universities in Tennessee, Michigan and Canada so much that they did a study of 139 Amish children to determine if modern technology is contributing to a growing obesity rate in other children.

The study published by the American College of Sports Medicine in 2007 showed that the Amish youth who participated had significantly higher levels of physical activity and very low rates of obesity.

The report found that the Amish boys averaged 17,174 steps per day; Amish girls 13,620. Pedometer scores of non-Amish children in elementary schools showed an average of about 12,000 steps per day, and the rates declined as the children aged.

The scientists found obesity rates among Amish children was 1.4 percent, according to the study. But the obesity rate among American boys and girls ages 6 to 19 is about 6.5 to 9.5 percent for boys and 6.6 to 11.7 percent for girls.

The study, authored by David R. Bassett Jr., a professor at the University of Tennessee–Knoxville, concluded that "assuming that the physical activity levels of these Amish youth resemble those of rural North American children 150 years ago, one can roughly estimate the effects of modernization on this important behavioral trait."

"When I grew up we didn't have a lot, but my parents taught us to work." –LaVern Schlabach

In an unscientific survey of 24 students age 6 to 11 at Meadowlark School near Arthur, the children talked about some of their typical daily activities. Here's what they do:

WORK ACTIVITIES	FUN ACTIVITIES	NIGHTTIME ACTIVITIES
feed the horses, cows, dogs, rabbits and/or chickens	trampolines	jigsaw puzzles
clean stalls in barn, manure in lots	softball	homework
help milk cows	volleyball	reading
mow	basketball	embroidery
weed the garden	(no organized leagues)	board games
wash dishes/set the table	rollerblading	crafts, like making cards with
babysit younger siblings	riding bicycles	stamps and ink pads
help with wash, hanging out	riding ponies	some parents allow
clothes, folding and putting away	shooting BB guns	battery-operated toys
help with canning, cooking	fishing	
help put up hay in barn	ice skating on ponds	
wash windows		
wash buggy		
gather eggs		
fill feeders in broiler houses		

Amish children wear clothes patterned after their parents. Even infants and toddlers are dressed in tiny replicas of the women's dresses and the men's pants and suspenders. Baby girls wear white crocheted bonnets or the white organdy covers like their mothers and big sisters.

Amish children do not attend movies, concerts, ball games, skating rinks or swimming pools. They do socialize with families and neighbors at sings and picnics, family reunions, weddings, funerals and other gatherings. It is unusual for Amish parents to hire a babysitter—the children go along.

Amish children speak Pennsylvania Dutch as their first language; they learn to read and write German in two-week summer schools. English is spoken in the Amish parochial schools.

Most Amish parents follow the adage, "Spare the rod, spoil the child," and spank for misbehavior. The slip of a cussword likely leads to a taste of soap.

Children do not participate in sports leagues, but they are eager to play softball, volleyball or basketball with siblings and neighbors.

"Most of us today still have agricultural roots. There's a lot of practical thinking and practical training in agriculture."
—Minister

Lots of Amish teens age 16 and up congregate on Saturday nights at the Amish community center on the south edge of Arthur to play volleyball. At times, 175 teens have shown up to play at 11 or 12 nets. Parents are chaperones. In the summertime, teens will gather for softball on Sunday afternoons.

Another group of 150 young people or more sometimes get together in smaller groups for softball or volleyball on other evenings at a school house or parents' home. They also plan "worker bees," to help someone in need weed a garden or other chores, and then play volleyball and have a snack afterward.

In most homes, Amish teens 13 to 15 are not allowed to run with their friends and would not be allowed to go out on Saturdays. Teenagers do not start dating until they are 16.

Amish teens can be baptized, take instruction and join the church at about the age of 16. Many parents then give the child his or her own horse and buggy.

After children leave school at eighth grade and begin working, they often give their paychecks to their parents until they marry or turn 21. The parents will give them a small allowance and bank the remainder until the child marries, when most parents help with the purchase of land, a house and/or starting a business.

When there is a death in the community, the Amish youth 16 and over will show up the evening before the funeral to sing hymns at the home where the funeral will be. As many as 300 to 500 "young folk" have shown up to sing; sometimes, the teens do not even know the deceased.

"I believe the agricultural setting is the best setting to raise a family in. The more urbanized things become the more you have kids running on the streets with idle time on their hands, which breeds problems." –Amish father

'Train a child in the way he should go …'

–Proverbs 22:6

*If Amish children
need special help,
there are a few schools
in the Amish community
to serve those needs.*

The bell in the belfry over the front door of Meadowlark School rings. It's 8:15 on a clear, sunny October morning.

Twenty or so Amish children, playing ball in a big, grassy lot behind the school, come running. The children have already put their ponies in the school-yard barn and parked the pony carts in a neat row outside. Some children have trekked alongside the country roads to get there. Some days, a few even rollerblade on the oil-chip roads.

Meadowlark School is one of 17 Amish parochial schools in the Arthur community. With its white siding and bell tower it looks true to Amish tradition—quaint, practical and simple. It has one large classroom for the 24 students and an outer room that is about the size of a double-car garage. The outer room is where

64

the children can have recess when the weather's bad. It's lined with cubbies for the jackets, the girls' black bonnets, the boys' straw hats and their lunch totes.

Teacher Marilyn Schrock has been teaching Amish children for 13 years. And like at all Amish parochial schools, the students call her by her first name. This year she has no eighth graders, and there are three times as many boys, 18, as girls, 6. Marilyn has hung pictures of apples in bushel baskets on which she's written the names of each student and the names of their mothers and fathers. There are 11 bushel baskets this year. All the children come from two-parent traditional homes, and all live nearby. They come from three neighboring church districts, and many are first- or second-cousins. Six of them are Marilyn's nieces and nephews. Because they are a tight community of neighbors and family, when there's an Amish wedding in the neighborhood (always on weekdays, not weekends), the school will close so the children can attend.

The children waste no time filing into the schoolhouse. They toss their ball gloves into their cubbies and enter the classroom without talking to take their seats at their desks.

Their entry is orderly, and quiet soon fills the room. Marilyn gives a nod, and a student leads the children, again single file, hymnbooks in hand, to the outer room. There they form three rows, the tallest children to the back.

They sing three hymns. The children take turns picking the hymns and that morning one of the young boys selected the recognizable "How Great Thou Art." Marilyn's clear soprano voice leads the children through the songs without benefit of a piano. They sing in English. Though Amish children speak Pennsylvania Dutch in their homes, the Amish leaders want the children to know and be comfortable with English. So school lessons are in English and children speak English even on the playground.

After the sing, Marilyn announces Marlin is turning 7 today. They sing the traditional "Happy Birthday" with a second verse that asks God for special blessings for Marlin that day. The children return single file to the classroom and stand by their desks. A child leads them in The Lord's Prayer, and they take their seats once more.

"How many disciples did Jesus have?" Marilyn asks.

A few raise their hands high. The one she calls on gets it correct—Jesus sent 70 other disciples out into the world. Marilyn reads a story about the disciples.

Five rows of students' desks crisscross the gleaming wood floors of the classroom. The ages of the children descend across the room from the oldest on the left to the youngest on the right.

With no electricity, the east and west walls are banked with windows, and the

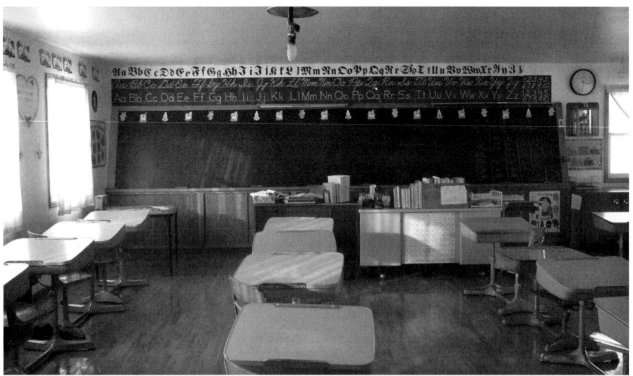

"A good example has twice the value of good advice." –Poster in Meadowlark School

Tuition is charged per family, rather than per child. According to one mother, tuition at her school was $1,000 a family. The amount of tuition varies from school to school and may depend on money earned through school fundraisers.

curtains—simple pastel blue cotton panels—are pulled back with a tie to let in the light. A handmade sign on the wall says "Praise the Lord for his goodness." Another says, "A good example has twice the value of good advice." Another quotes the Golden Rule.

Marilyn, 44, is wearing the traditional Amish collarless dress, this one in a polyester and Wedgwood blue. She wears black stockings and dark tennis shoes. The thin, white ribbons of her white head covering are tied loosely.

The Amish schoolgirls also wear white or black head coverings, their hair pulled back into buns at the nape of their necks. Their mothers make the caps of sheer organdy and treat them with starch to make them hold their pleats and shape. They wear their "coverings," as they're called, all day. The colors of the girls' homemade dresses are muted and dark, like a dusty plum or dark teal. They wear black stockings and dark tennis or tie-up shoes. The boys wear collared shirts in pastel shades of yellow, blue and green. Most are homemade. The boys have dark suspenders attached to the polyester-cotton blend denim pants made by their mothers. After she's finished reading the book about Jesus' disciples, Marilyn sets a kitchen timer for 5 minutes.

"Does anyone have any news to share?" she asks.

One girl tells about a man knocking on their door late at night, scaring them at first. But he stopped to tell them their cow was out on the road.

"OH! Was it your cow?" Marilyn asks.

"No, the neighbor's," the girl sighed.

A young boy said he heard a car hit a buggy in Arthur the day before. Marilyn asks if anyone knows anything about it. One of the older boys reports that he heard the buggy was ruined, but the driver was OK and he walked the horse home. He's not sure whose buggy it was; several children enthusiastically nod in agreement to Marilyn's reflection that no one was seriously hurt.

At 8:45, they turn their attention to Psalm 56, verses 4 and 5. The older children write in a notebook they keep especially for the Bible passages. The younger children copy a shorter, simpler verse.

Once finished, Marilyn or her teaching assistant, Lori Otto, check the students' spelling and grammar.

As they start their school work, Marilyn and Lori move between grade levels. The first graders are learning words that start with B. Older students work at a table on math with Lori. Another group of middle grade children study time zones. "If it's 5 p.m. in Hawaii, what time is it in St. John's Newfoundland?" Sunlight pours into the room through the east windows, but on gloomy days there are two propane ceiling lights. There is also a propane floor lamp if needed.

When the clock on the wall registers 9:45, Marilyn taps a bell and the students put away their work. She reads the names of a couple of students and they leave for recess first. They are the batters.

At recess, a few of the youngest girls head for the swings and teeter-totter, but most of the children play a game where a batter hits balls to the fielders; once a fielder's caught three, the fielder becomes the batter.

The 15-minute recess ends with Marilyn ringing a hand-held school bell. Students stop to get a drink of water, and a few of the boys remove their shoes and socks and enter the classroom in bare feet; it's getting warmer.

First order of business after recess is the recitation one more time of Psalm 56, verses 4 and 5.

"In God I will praise his word, in God I have put my trust; I will not fear what flesh can do unto me. Every day they wrest my words; all their thoughts are against me for evil."

The youngest children have a simple line from Psalm 119 to recite: "The entrance of his word giveth light."

Then it's more reading, class assignments and tests. The third graders work

About 75 Amish children go into the Arthur public schools for elementary school. The Amish children in the elementary grades are in the same classrooms with non-Amish children, but are excused from movies and using computers if the parents request it. But the older Amish children, those in seventh- and eighth-grades, are in self-contained classrooms with public school teachers. They learn reading, writing, arithmetic and life skills. Some may learn to type on computers or study science, unless a parent objects.

subtraction problems on the blackboard; Lori tests other children with math flash cards.

Amish schools focus on reading, writing and arithmetic, and also teach social studies and health. There is no sex education, but lots of information on farm safety. They don't study science, art or music. They do commit to memory scores of hymns by the time they leave school.

Students at the Amish parochial schools take field trips with a flat wagon, straw bales for seating and horsepower.

The Amish leaders often hear criticism about the decision to limit education to eight grades, but they point out that though the classroom work ends the education continues. The children learn trades and homemaking skills, and they learn the ethics of working and responsibility.

At 11, one of the sixth grade girls leaves the classroom to put the hot lunch items children brought into the gas oven in the outer room.

By 11:30, when Marilyn dismisses the children to get their lunches, the casserole leftovers and stews are hot. When the children return to the classroom with their lunches, they stand beside their desks and wait until Marilyn is ready to lead them in a prayer: "Thank you for the food we eat—thank you for the friends we meet—thank you for the work and play—thank you God for this happy day."

Those without soups and leftover casseroles eat sandwiches—typically with meat and cheese and just one slice of bread. Only one child that day eats a bag of potato chips—all the other foods the children bring are home-cooked. They drink milk or juice from insulated jugs; there are no bottles or packaged juices, Gatorade or soft drinks. Some enjoy cakes and cookies for dessert. Fruit, too.

Casual conversation over lunch includes talk among some of the older boys about a tractor they've seen parked at the sale barn that had a GPS on it. One child tells Marilyn about a new horse, another child asks Marilyn if she's heard about the neighbors' new baby being born. One boy tells about his father's weekend trip to Indiana to see his brother ordained a minister.

With recess ahead, the children don't dally over their lunches, but quickly pack them away so they can go outside. When Marilyn gives the word, all but a few get their ball gloves and head to the ball diamond. The remaining ones wipe the desks clean.

"Today we gathered nuts and raked leaves. So we had a bunch of fun." –Journal entry at Bear Creek School

The ball diamond has a homemade backstop and the bases are metal discs from a farm implement. Every child plays ball. The teams are reassigned every nine innings.

Marilyn and Lori grab their gloves and head for the diamond, too. They're the pitchers, and uniformed in their dresses and head coverings, they catch line drives and throw to second base to stop a runner, enjoying the game as much as the children. When the youngest children are at bat, one of the older students stands with his arms wrapped around the little one to help swing the bat. Likewise, an older child will hold a young one's hand while they run the bases together.

It's clear the noon recess game is the highlight of the day as the children giggle and relax waiting their turns. But no one yells a catcall of any kind to the batters or the fielders. There is no argument when a runner and the ball meet at first base at the same time. There are no disputes over the strikes or balls.

One 9-year-old boy, disappointed because his team has made three outs without scoring, takes his position on the field and says, "C'mon! We got to get busy and get some runs next time."

His attempt to urge his team on doesn't sit well with Marilyn. She mildly suggests that if he doesn't want to have the right attitude, he can finish recess in the schoolhouse. He doesn't egg his team on again.

As the children grow warm, more peel off their shoes and socks to run the bases barefoot. They also bat without batting helmets.

*School district expenses
include the teacher's salary
(which would not
include retirement or
insurance benefits),
purchase of textbooks
and workbooks,
a tank of propane
for heating and lighting,
and occasional cleaning and
paper supplies.*

At 12:30, recess is over and the mostly barefoot children take their seats again. Marilyn reads the class a story; they recite the Bible verse from Psalm 56 one more time. The fourth graders take an English test while others do assigned lessons in workbooks.

Marilyn hears a siren on the road outside the school. It passes and heads south. Marilyn excuses herself to go outside and see if she can see where it's going.

She returns and tells the children the ambulance headed way on down south, so it didn't go to one of their homes.

"It's scary to see an ambulance," Marilyn says, "but we have to be pleased that someone is getting the help they need." She directs her comments toward the younger side of the classroom. "If you get scared," she says, "close your eyes and say a little prayer for the people that need the help. That will help you get rid of your fear."

By 2, some children who have been assigned sweep the wood floor and shake the rugs. Some days, children also muck out the barn.

More lessons, more recitations, more flash cards, assignments noted on the board, and papers handed in and school dismisses at 3:15.

The children collect their lunch boxes and head for home on foot or get the ponies out of the barn and hitch up to the pony carts. Typically, the oldest child gets to drive the cart, and with large Amish families as many as five can pile in. Neighbors hitch rides, too.

Marilyn stands at the road, watching for cars and trucks, making sure it's safe for the pony carts to pull onto the road. The boys in their straw hats and the girls with black bonnets over the top of their head coverings leave the schoolyard knowing when they get home they'll change out of their good clothes into play clothes, get a snack and then do chores. There are no daycare centers in the Amish community; Amish mothers do not work outside the home.

The children in Meadowlark were very well-behaved, respectful and quiet. They kept themselves occupied in the classroom and didn't seem tempted to goof off. They showed concern for one another. And their manners on the ball field were impeccable. The older children didn't get frustrated or whine as the young ones fumbled balls and took too many swings. And even when a batter hit the ball over the fence, few clapped or cheered. Scoring runs didn't seem important.

The children appeared to be more appreciative of being outside on a nice fall day and getting to take off their shoes and socks and go barefoot. A simple pleasure, for sure, at a one-room country school on a sunny October day.

It's also important to point out that the school visit took place one week to the day after the tragic murder of five young Amish girls in the country schoolhouse at Nickel Mines, Pa., on Oct. 2, 2006.

The timing was not of my choosing—I'd talked to Marilyn about spending a day in her school before the shootings. I would have understood if she had decided to back out. But Marilyn graciously let her invitation stand and I— an "English" lady in a pickup truck with a notebook and a ball-point pen—sat at the back of the classroom taking copious notes, smiling a lot.

I wanted to assure the children that though I was a stranger, I was harmless. Some of the littlest ones looked at me with wide eyes and I hoped it was not because their view of the outside world had changed in a week's time. Neither Marilyn nor the children mentioned the shootings, but the Bible verses the children studied that day addressed fear.

"What time I am afraid I will trust in thee. In God I will praise his work. In God I have put my trust. I will not fear what flesh can do unto me."

Marilyn said weeks later that she did indeed select Bible verses after the shooting to assure the children. A month later, the verse they were learning was from Matthew 6—about forgiveness.

The day after the shooting in Pennsylvania, one of the Amish bishops visited the school to talk with them. Of course, the children were upset, and after Marilyn and the children talked about it, she decided they needed to move on.

"Thank you for the food we eat—thank you for the friends we meet—thank you for the work and play—thank you God for this happy day." –Prayer before lunch

"I said, 'If we keep talking about this it's going to be harder for us to trust, and it'll reopen our fears. You can discuss it at home, but let's try not to talk about it much here.'"

She said she tries not to think about the shooting or let it affect how she conducts school. There have been no changes made.

"You know, if someone wanted to, they could drive by and shoot everyone while we're outside playing. So (worrying) doesn't do any good," Marilyn said. "I like to trust people, I guess." She sighs. "I just don't know."

Hundreds of editorials were written around the country saying that the Amish taught us all a lesson about forgiveness and true Christianity because the Amish at Nickel Mines had visited the killer's widow and children. Some of the victims' parents even attended the killer's funeral.

"That's the way we were taught," she said. "And to us, if we don't forgive we aren't true to our faith."

Marilyn, a profoundly devout Amish lady raised in the home of one of the community's senior ministers, hopes she could be as forgiving.

"I guess I wonder if my faith would be strong enough that I could do what they're doing out there," she said.

She knows some people have questioned why God would let that tragedy happen. Marilyn doesn't know if He did or not, but she is sure that if God did let that happen, those five little girls are with Him now.

"And they are not living in fear with him," she said. "They are not in fear now."

Note: In the summer of 2007, the fathers of Meadowlark School raised the roof and added a second story to the school. Growing numbers of children for fall 2007 prompted the expansion to a two-room school.

State regulations require 160 days of schooling a year. The Amish school year typically runs from late August through late April or early May. They observe Thanksgiving, Christmas and Easter but no other school holidays.

Families of the students at Bear Creek school gather at the two-room schoolhouse on a misty April morning for the end-of-school program.

I park my pickup truck on the side of the road and walk past the church wagon and a line of buggies parked in the back lot to search for Rachel Schrock, one of the two school teachers. She is playing volleyball with the children on a concrete volleyball court, while the families of the children are mingling in the yard and inside the school.

It's a big crowd for the program—maybe 100 or more turn out to see the 32 children sing and recite poems. It's a weekday morning, and I'm struck by how many men took off work to be there. I mention that to Susie Schrock, Rachel's mother, who's volunteered to be my guide that day. Some are self-employed, she said, but if they work for an Amish factory, it's understood that they need time off to attend an important school event like the spring program.

The two-room schoolhouse has been converted into one large room for the program. The wooden wall separating the rooms has been removed and stored for the day. The desks have been pushed into a corner. The long wooden benches from the church wagon fill the room.

A few rows are set aside for the school children. I sat in the middle near Susie and with the other women who were grandmothers, sisters, aunts, cousins and neighbors of the children. Many mothers had their youngest children in tow, even infants, and all sat on the benches quietly waiting for the program to start. Another section of benches was for the men. Some fathers had their toddler sons sitting alongside.

Just a few weeks before, I'd spent the entire day at Bear Creek in Rachel's class of fourth- through eighth-graders. I'd been amazed at how well-behaved the children were, at how the day's regimen ran like clockwork and how much respect they showed for Rachel, who is 22. I never saw her give one of those warning looks that teachers are adept at, and I was impressed by how athletic she was on the ball field at noon recess.

At the program as we waited for the children to file in this day, I also noticed no one was talking or whispering. I thought about the public school events I'd been to for my own children and remember there being a loud buzz of conversation just before the shushes came and the program got under way. No need for shushing at the Amish school.

The program began with a hymn, led by a male singer at the back of the room. The slow hymn, sung in German, was about God's creations and the beauty of the coming spring and summer, I learned later. The adults sang four or five verses as the children took their seats on the benches.

Then the children rose in unison and walked single file to the front of the room and made four rows, the oldest to the back. Rachel and the other teacher took their places in the back row and sang with the children.

After singing a song called "Gratitude" and another called "This Life Is Hard To Understand," the first-graders began a recitation.

The poems were spoken in unison, and then each child took a turn reciting a stanza solo. They'd spent weeks memorizing the words.

All the recitations had religious or moral themes. The first-graders spoke about taking the time to be nice to your parents and friends. Some older children told in a poem the story of the little Dutch Boy who put his finger in the dike to save his town. Older children recited a poem about a young man who went to the draft board to seek conscientious objector status. (The Amish people will serve in the military but not in combat.)

During the school program, a few fathers spoke to the children in German about setting goals and making the right choices, admonishing them to stay on the right path. There were prayers, when all went to their knees, their faces to the benches.

The five eighth-graders were marking the end of their classroom education, but they received no special recognition in the program. Rachel said later she gave each of the eighth-graders framed graduation certificates and a harmonica. She said the children likely received new homemade shirts and dresses for the program from their parents, but probably not any other gifts.

And I also didn't see any of the Amish parents or family members looking at the children with rapt attention or pride. So often in my own life, I beamed when my children were in a school program. I know I'd have watched them sing and recite without taking my eyes off them, smiling at their brilliance, proud of their

Amish schoolteachers have eighth-grade educations but do have monthly meetings to share information and concerns about curriculum and teaching methods, and annual regional conferences with other Amish teachers.

Once a week, one of the ministers, bishops or one of the children's fathers will come to school for devotions. Typically, they tell or read a Bible story with a moral lesson and discuss it with the children.

accomplishment. But a strong principle in the Amish faith is not to be proud, and during the program I noticed the parents and grandparents did not make adoring looks while their children were reciting and singing. I didn't hear any grandparents gushing about what a great job a child had done.

After the program ended, everyone went downstairs for a potluck lunch. Susie had brought an extra plate for me and I helped myself to meatballs, mashed potatoes, sweet potato casserole, corn and green beans and a few types of Jell-o salad and a brownie and a slice of pie, and oh, is that cheesecake?

The wooden benches had been stacked on top of each other to make tables, and I soon noticed that the women around me were scraping their plates with their spoons, getting every last morsel. I looked at the heaps of food I'd served myself and realized I could never eat it all.

I knew that the thrifty Amish people believe in cleaning their plates and would not approve of me wasting food. I tried to eat it all before admitting to Susie my embarrassment. She laughed, and I learned a lesson.

After the meal, the ball game between the fathers and the boys got under way, even though it was drizzling rain. The girls played volleyball and some younger children played a game called King Base. The parents and other family members mingled.

I left with new clarity about how the Amish faith shows itself in the importance of family and community. The school program took a few hours, but it drew not only parents but grandparents, sisters, brothers, aunts and uncles and neighbors together.

It included time for worship and thanks to God but no frills, frou-frou, bells or whistles, armloads of gifts, gushing, or any outward show of pride about whose child might be the brightest or smartest or cutest.

Like so much that's Amish, it was plain and simple and satisfying. Not a lot heaped on a plate. But enough to get the job done, nicely.

How long does it take to hitch a pony to the cart? "Five to 10 minutes. If you fiddle, it takes 15." –Clarence, 12

Students in Rachel Schrock's fourth- through eighth-grade class at Bear Creek School took turns writing in a class journal. Here are excerpts from the 2006-07 school year.

It was dreary most of the day today. This morning it misted and at last recess it started to rain. We played volleyball today.

Now the seventh and eighth grades are going to sweep the classroom. The sixth grade girls are going to sweep the entrances. Rachel told Jesse and Wilbur to beat the rugs.

Since it's too cold to play softball everyone played Dogs & Rabbits.

Mary Lorene put the hot stuff into the stove today.

The eighth-graders from last year came and we played ball 'till it was time to go home. The board members brought lunch and the children brought finger foods.

Today was warm and sunny and we also got to go barefoot.

Today we gathered nuts and raked leaves so we had a bushel of fun.

Today was a fine day to go out and play in the mud. We played Dogs & Rabbits at first recess and went skating on the ice at noon. The ice was not all quite hard enough to play on.

It was really cold. The little girls stayed in to play with their dolls.

We played in the snow all the recesses. Most of us had a snowball fight. Neil brought his pony and gave rides to whoever wanted one.

Daryl Kaufman was here to give sled rides.

I got to swing high. I jumped out to see how far I could fly.

Today we had blab school but then Rachel said we have to quit making monkeyshines.

Rachel got a sewing basket for her birthday.

'Dear children ... flee far away from ... sin'

–Amish hymn

Dating among Amish teens includes no movie dates or concerts. Amish teens would likely meet at a Saturday night volleyball game at the Otto Center, and the boy would take the girl home in his buggy. Or they might meet at a Sunday afternoon softball game or evening sing, and again he would give her a ride home.

The Amish teens are not allowed to date until they are 16.

Once a couple begins to date steadily, they would go together to church and family activities, like birthday parties, reunions and weddings.

One Amish mother said it would be very unusual for a dating couple to see each other more than a few times a week.

Unmarried Amish couples do not live together.

There have been some babies born to single mothers, but in the Amish community if the girl regrets the behavior and makes her peace with God, all is forgiven and she and the baby are accepted into the community. "Youth are expected to date openly, and to avoid sensual or close bodily contact," a minister said.

Some single Amish in their late teens and early 20s migrate in the winter months to Pinecraft, an Amish settlement near Sarasota, Fla. Pinecraft draws Amish from settlements all over the country, and the young people can get jobs in the restaurant and hotel industry, make new friends and possibly meet Mr. or Miss Right.

Some teens raised in Amish homes, but not yet baptized into the church, are under no jurisdiction from church leaders. Because they live at home, they might dress in the Amish clothes and get around with horses and buggies, but these teens are sometimes seen in public smoking, wearing makeup, drinking, using radios in their buggies or behaving in other ways that break the Amish Ordnung (rules). Once the teens join the church they could be shunned, meaning other Amish church members would not associate with them or eat with them, or excommunicated. Amish teens and young adults usually make sure they are ready to commit to the restrictions before they take the important step of joining the church.

"In courting, he would take her everywhere she wants to go. Everywhere she'd go, he'd take her. Family reunions. Birthday parties. Things like that." –Minister

Amish teens cannot socialize without their parents until the age of 16.

Rumspringa. A word in Pennsylvania Dutch that loosely translated means running around or running free.

It's a word that's become commonly known among many non-Amish as television shows and movies have focused on the wild side of Amish teens, and it's caused confusion and misunderstandings between the non-Amish and those of the Amish faith, and even some within the Amish community itself.

Outsiders have heard that when Amish teens turn 16, their parents pack their bags, give their blessing and tell them to go out and get a taste of the world—run free, be wild and get it out of your system.

But raise that image to some Amish church leaders and you'll get a shriek like you've touched a raw nerve.

"Where on earth did you ever get that idea? Where's that stuff come from?" Nothing could be further from the truth, the church leaders say. No Amish parent tells their child to go out and drink and smoke and run wild and do drugs.

It may seem like that to outsiders because they are probably seeing Amish teens who still live at home with their parents who do run on the wild side. Some may own or drive trucks or cars. Some experiment with alcohol and drugs. A few have been involved in crime. But these teens are not church members so they are not under the jurisdiction of the church laws. Once a teen or young adult is baptized and becomes a church member, they need to obey the church laws or they could be shunned or excommunicated.

"*The Amish have large families and retain a high percentage of their youth.*"
–Walter Beachy

"The outsiders see us and they see our young folks out there driving trucks and things and they think our kids are wild, but that's not 100 percent of our young folk," a bishop said. "They see the ones who are out there, but the ones who are behaving are the ones you don't see. So yes, even though we have that element amongst us, we also have an element that doesn't. Thank God," he said.

Part of the misunderstanding by the non-Amish is probably tied to the word rumspringa. It does mean run loose, and once a teen is 16, the teen is considered of age. Being of age means that the Amish parents will allow the teens to socialize and date.

In the teen years between 13 and 16, teenagers are not allowed to socialize. They can't go to youth sings or the Sunday afternoon softball games or any other activities without their parents.

Parents often buy their teenagers their own horse and buggy.

But at 16 they are given that freedom to participate on their own. On a Sunday afternoon in the summertime, one can see these 16-and-up teenagers at the ball diamond behind the Arthur High School—bleachers filled with teenage girls watching the guys play softball. The Saturday night volleyball at the Otto Center and the Sunday sings are for those 16 and up, too.

One Amish housewife said she couldn't wait until she turned 16 because she wanted to take part in the youth sings. Little brothers and sisters don't even get to tag along. Sweet 16 is a birthday looked forward to for that step toward independence.

State laws allow the teens at 16 to start working in shops and factories. Once they're getting a little income and meeting others their world expands and some begin experimenting with alcohol and drugs, and Amish parents search for ways to prevent it.

A very few Amish parents might look away, but most parents struggle with the challenges of teenagers, a bishop said.

"Most parents of rebels feel at wit's end and have shed many tears because of the rebellion of their youth," said a minister.

The Amish do not believe in baptizing until the teen is about 16, and many are baptized and join in the later teens and early 20s.

Talking to parents within the community, it's easy to detect the frustration they faced raising their own teenagers. One Amish man, 28, admitted that he did do some running with friends before he joined the church and got married, and he did some things he wasn't proud of. But he never owned a truck and he's never yet tasted beer.

He said he was raised by his parents to be Amish, and when he faced temptations he thought about his parents. He didn't want to let them down.

The Amish teens who have had pickup trucks *and* lived at home created all kinds of problems for the parents. Not just within the home but with Amish neighbors who object to such things as well. But there are some happy endings—a rebel will find a nice Amish girl, sell the truck, join the church and settle down into traditional family life. A minister said the church teaches and prefers the young people make peace with the Lord—their creator—first, and then in faith search for a lifetime partner.

"If I don't teach my children to work, I've not done my duty."
–Ben Graber

"Most Amish youth expect to one day be married and have a family of their own," the minister said. "A few choose to be single and most realize that happiness in life does not depend on marriage or singlehood, but a good relationship with their savior and being a respectable citizen in their community."

Church leaders estimate that 85 to 90 percent of their young people make the decision to join the church.

Unmarried Amish couples
do not live together.

Dating among Amish teens includes no movie dates or concerts. Amish teens would likely meet at a Saturday night volleyball game at the Otto Center, and the boy would take the girl home in his buggy. Or they might meet at a Sunday afternoon softball game or evening sing, and again he would give her a ride home.

Once a couple begins to date steadily, they would go together to church and family activities, like birthday parties, reunions and weddings.

One Amish mother said it would be very unusual for a dating couple to see each other more than a few times a week.

There have been some babies born to single mothers, but in the Amish community if the girl regrets the behavior and makes her peace with God, all is forgiven and she and the baby are accepted into the community.

"Youth are expected to date openly, and to avoid sensual or close bodily contact," a minister said.

Some single Amish in their late teens and early 20s migrate in the winter months to Pinecraft, an Amish settlement near Sarasota, Fla. Pinecraft draws Amish from settlements all over the country, and the young people can get jobs in the restaurant and hotel industry, make new friends and possibly meet Mr. or Miss Right.

Some teens raised in Amish homes, but not yet baptized into the church, are under no jurisdiction from church leaders. Because they live at home, they might dress in the Amish clothes and get around with horses and buggies, but these teens are sometimes seen in public smoking, wearing makeup, drinking, using radios in their buggies or behaving in other ways that break the Amish Ordnung (rules). Once the teens join the church they could be shunned, meaning other Amish church members would not associate with them or eat with them, or excommunicated. Amish teens and young adults usually make sure they are ready to commit to the restrictions before they take the important step of joining the church.

'… join our hands, our hearts, our lives in the Lord'

—prayer

S ue Ann Plank and William Yoder greet their wedding guests with a friendly handshake as they arrived for the 9 a.m. wedding service at Sue Ann's parents' home south of Arthur.

The 350 or so guests had parked their horses and buggies in a nearby pasture, and those planning to stay until evening took the additional step of unhitching their horses and putting them in the barn.

It's a Friday in March to accommodate guests coming in from out of state.

Because the Plank home is filled with tables set for the wedding meal, the church service is held in a storage shed—emptied and scrubbed clean days before—behind the hardware store owned by the bride's parents, Howard and Mary Plank.

The guests and their children sit quietly on wooden benches, men in one section and women another, waiting for the Vorsinger (song leader) to begin with the opening hymn. The hymns and sermons are conducted in High German, rather than the Pennsylvania Dutch the Amish use in their daily life.

Horses of wedding guests are unhitched and put out to pasture or in the barn because weddings typically last all day, with a noon and evening meal served and lots of singing and visiting.

81

As the singing gets under way, the couple meets with the ministers and bishop back at the home, a short walk from the shed. The church leaders talk to the couple about the seriousness of marriage, and how in God's eyes the two will now become one.

The first two or three hymns take 30 minutes, followed by the entry of the ministers, bishop and the couple. Sue Ann and William and their four witnesses—two men and two women called "nava hockers" in Dutch—sit on chairs, facing each other before the minister as he gives his sermon. In most Amish weddings, the sermons focus on what the Scriptures say about marriage.

Because the Amish believe that one should not draw attention to oneself and that everyone, rich and poor, should look alike and be equal, there are no bouquets, ribbons or decorations for the service. Those are unnecessary frills that would present the temptation to try to make one wedding more special than another. Amish weddings follow the same template, set pretty much in stone, as the tradition has passed down through the generations.

The guests arrived in their Sunday best, as they would at any church service, the men dressed in white shirts and black trousers and the women in their dresses, capes, aprons and head covers.

Sue Ann wears a navy blue dress, white cape and apron that she had made, and a black organdy head cover that her two sisters-in-law had worn at their weddings. She'll not box the dress away as a keepsake; it will become her new Sunday dress for church and others' weddings. The black organdy head cover might be worn by another sister-in-law at her wedding.

"The cake was white with dark blue roses and it was heart-shaped. Two layers I think. Chocolate and vanilla both. The top had a cluster of the icing roses." –Sue Ann Plank

William wears a white shirt, black trousers and a black jacket called a mutzi.

The two female witnesses, Sue Ann's sister and a close friend, wear the same color dress as Sue Ann, made with fabric that Sue Ann had given them.

The service at a wedding takes two-and-half-hours, like most Amish church services do, and the wedding ceremony comes at the end. Bishop Daniel Chupp, Sue Ann's uncle, asks them each the questions reserved for weddings.

In German, the bishop asks William: "Do you solemnly promise your wife that if she should be afflicted with bodily weakness, sickness or some such circumstance that you will care for her as is fitting a Christian husband?"

He asks the same question of Sue Ann.

Then the bishop asks both: "Do you solemnly promise with one another that you will love and bear and be patient with one another, and not separate from each other until the dear God shall part you from each other through death?"

After prayers, the bishop instructs the couple to join hands.

"The God of Abraham, the God of Isaac, and the God of Jacob be with you, and help you come together and shed His blessing richly upon you, and this through Jesus Christ, Amen."

A final hymn is sung.

A light rain falls as Sue Ann and William and the witnesses head into the house. As the guests filter in for the noon meal, Sue Ann and her witnesses change from their black organdy head covers into white ones.

As a married woman, Sue Ann's head cover for church will be white, and as a married man, William will grow a beard around his jawline.

Months later, Sue Ann, a tall, attractive woman with blue eyes, still smiles talking about her wedding day. She sat in the shade outside the small house she and William rent south of Arthur, recalling that while some of it seemed to be a blur, a lot she does remember.

She and William will eat the top of their three-layer wedding cake for their first anniversary. She's not working in a cabinet shop anymore, but is busy taking care of a large garden and canning. And now that she's been through her own wedding, she'll help her friends and other relatives when they need help with future weddings.

WEDDING SHOPPING LIST

MASHED POTATOES FOR 100
(You'd need about four batches for a typical wedding)

30 pounds of potatoes
2 quarts milk
cup salt
cup butter
1 cup sour cream

SALISBURY STEAK FOR 60
(You'd need at least six batches)

15 pounds hamburger
12 eggs
5 cups chopped onions
7 cups milk
14 cups cracker crumbs
6 teaspoons salt
3 teaspoons pepper
14 10-ounce cans of mushroom soup

DRESSING FOR 100
(You'd need about four batches)

60 pieces bread
5 sticks celery
10 cups chicken broth
5 cups boiling water
2 cups butter
15 eggs
5 tablespoons chicken seasoning
salt to taste
2 cups milk

When a couple has a lot of relatives and friends with children in a particular school, the school will likely close for the day so the children and teachers can attend their wedding.

Some Amish families have large tents put up near the house for the church-wedding service so the meal can be served in their home.

A typical Amish wedding that includes two meals for as many as 500 guests will cost the bride's family $3,000-$4,000. The largest expense is the food.

Imagine serving a sit-down meal to 350 to 450 people in your home at midday and then serving another 300 in the evening.

That's exactly what Amish families do for their daughters' weddings.

When Naomi Schrock married Chester Mast, they seated 373 in her parents' home—on the first floor and in the basement—and another 70 in her married sister's house next door.

"There's no such thing as a small Amish wedding," an Amish minister laughed. "We have families!"

Once a couple decides to marry, the minister makes the announcement in church. The couple will mail written invitations to those who live away, but they will spend the next several days traveling together in horse and buggy around the community inviting local guests in person.

The bride's mother and the bride also ask about 30 to 40 sisters, cousins, aunts, neighbors and friends to serve as cooks; the couple asks about 40 young people to serve as wait staff for the wedding meals.

A few weeks before the wedding, friends come to help move furniture out of the bride's parents' home and clean the house from top to bottom. Sam and Susie Schrock, Naomi's parents, moved nearly all their day-to-day furniture to the second floor of their large farmhouse. Rental tables snaked around the now-bare first floor with wooden benches from the church wagon. The first floor sat 201. Tables set up in the basement seated 172. Another 70 were seated in the house next door.

There were also wait stations interspersed among the tables to hold the coffee, water jugs, soapy tubs of water, fresh linens, pies and the serving dishes.

The Saturday before the Wednesday wedding, Naomi and her sisters, cousins and friends set all the tables with dishes, silverware, water glasses, cups and saucers, and pretty dishes for pickles and condiments. The Amish don't approve of frills but do allow themselves paper napkins engraved with the names of the bride, groom and wedding date. The church wagon provides dishes, glasses and silverware, but Susie Schrock and her three married daughters and daughters-in-law were able to pool enough of their good dishes—with a pink rose pattern—for all the tables on the first floor. Once set, the tables were draped with sheets to protect them until the wedding.

One special corner table on the first floor is for the bride, groom and the four witnesses. It is draped with a royal blue tablecloth, and also holds a small wedding cake, usually two layers, with icing decorations. In keeping with the Amish preference to keep weddings simple with few temptations for one-upmanship, there are no flowers, decorations or cake toppers.

A few days before the wedding, the 30 to 40 relatives and friends who've been asked to be cooks arrive to spend the days preparing the meals. The Amish families rent cooking and cooling wagons—trailers brought in with gas stoves, sinks, refrigerators, freezers, large bowls, pots and pans—to prepare the feast.

The menu for the noon meal includes Salisbury steak, mashed potatoes and gravy, dressing, Jell-o salad, lettuce salad, corn, homemade bread, peanut butter pie and pecan pie.

After the wedding, the bride and couple lead the guests into the house; the close family is seated closest to the couple. The wait staff serve the meal from their wait stations. If there is a very large crowd, the guests will eat in shifts, with the wait staff washing the dishes and re-setting the tables in between.

Of course, prayers are said before and after the meal. And when the dishes are cleared, singing begins.

Most of the afternoon is spent singing hymns with wedding themes. Some of the guests might return to their homes at that time.

Friends of the bride will have opened the gifts, which would be on display. They are practical items to begin a household, and some are even wrapped in dish and bath towels rather than wedding paper. They likely include

mixing bowls, skillets, bed pillows, a set of glassware, a small drying rack for laundry, potholders, dish towels and garden tools. Many Amish mothers will give their daughters three quilts to start their household with—a pieced quilt, an embroidered quilt and a coverlet.

The Amish tend to spend $25 to $50 on wedding gifts, but some co-workers often go together on a large gift, such as a gas grill. In some families, the couple receives a piece of furniture from their parents—a couch or a recliner.

One practical tradition in the community is that a week or so after a wedding, friends will often have a grocery shower to help fill the couple's pantry.

About 4 p.m., the cooks and wait staff will begin gearing up to serve those guests remaining at 5 p.m. The menu at Naomi and Chester's evening meal featured baked ham, rather than Salisbury steak, and the pecan pie came with ice cream, but the rest of the menu was the same as the noon meal.

Once those guests have eaten, the tables are cleared and dishes washed

"I made my dress. Dark blue. I had a white cape and apron. I'll keep on wearing that."
–Sue Ann Plank

The couple keeps their wedding plans secret, except for close family and friends, until the announcement is made at church.

It's not uncommon for a wedding service to be held in a barn—scrubbed clean and sprayed for flies in the weeks beforehand. The meal would then be served in the house.

Many families plan ahead for weddings by planting extra sweet corn or green beans or by butchering an extra steer or pig for the wedding meals.

and some of the oldest guests will likely return home.

About 6:30, the young friends of the couple begin arriving after work. They'll get an evening meal of baked ham and all the trimmings. The evening ends with the young folk singing songs to the bride and groom until about 10 p.m.

The bride and groom spend their first night together in the bride's home. They get up early the next morning and help with the cleanup. Sometimes it takes days to get all the dishes and tables put away, the church wagons loaded, the cook wagons cleaned and the furniture

returned so that life is back to normal at the bride's parents' home.

The bride and groom give their wait staff and witnesses gifts called trophies. They are often useful items the couple made themselves, such as an oak napkin holder, carved with the wedding date and names of the bride and groom. The cooks might get a pretty platter and a dish towel.

At Sue Ann Plank's and William Yoder's wedding, the wedding program listed more than 100 names, thanking them for their help with the wedding.

"Mom and dad have to let go. That doesn't mean they don't care. But they have to let (the married couple) be a family." –Bishop

'… Going home with Jesus'

–hymn

In the Amish community, the word "neighbor" is used as a verb—as in, do you know the Hochstetlers? Yes, we *neighbor* with them.

That spirit of dropping what you're doing when your neighbor needs help is never more evident than when a member of the Amish community dies.

Without waiting to be asked, the neighbors immediately go to the home of the deceased and begin making the arrangements for the wake and funeral. They don't need to trouble the immediate family members, who might still be at the hospital, as they make arrangements for the large tent to be erected at the home of the deceased. The church wagons with the wooden benches and hymn books, plastic glassware, cooking pots and utensils begin arriving. A refrigerator trailer arrives to hold the hams, noodles, casseroles, salads, soups, pies and other dishes that will be brought in over the next three days.

Neighbor women roll up their sleeves and get to work in the kitchen, bringing in huge coffee urns, coffee cups, trays, paper plates and setting up tables to serve the food buffet-style to the crowds of mourners. Someone makes signs—buggy parking, car parking—and the men empty sheds and scrub them out to seat the crowd that can number from 500 to 2,000 or more. Large battery-operated fans are also brought in; porta potties delivered. Neighbors create parking lots in pastures and

Neighbors or extended family will stay with the coffin around the clock until burial, once it's delivered to the home.

hayfields, stringing large, heavy wires for the horses and buggies to be tied to. Big water jugs are filled with ice and drinking water.

The Amish people do have their loved ones embalmed at the local funeral home, but once the body is returned to the deceased's home for the wake and funeral, the family and neighbors are its caretakers and take full responsibility for the body. The coffin often sits in an emptied room in the house, and family friends take turns staying with the body night and day until the burial. If the coffin needs to be moved, the family or pallbearers pick it up and take it to the tent or shed or another room in the house.

The Amish have their own plain cemeteries with all the stones identical in size, color and information. The four pallbearers dig the graves themselves, and they erect a small canopy over the grave site.

"Our children are taken to funerals and visitations from the time they are little babies and up. They come face to face with death. They know it's a fact of life—that there's no guarantee how long we're going to be here." –Minister

Friends and family start arriving to pay their respects and meet the family soon after the body is delivered to the home and the coffin has been placed for viewing.

Throughout the day, the numbers are sparse enough that people can talk and mingle with family members to express their sympathies. But in the late afternoons and evenings, when the numbers increase, there is an unspoken rule that the line must keep moving; talking with the family of the deceased is not allowed in the line. So the mourners wait in a long snake of a line, sometimes close to an hour or more, pass by the coffin and then give the immediate family members a simple handshake. No hugs, no conversations. Just handshakes.

Typically, the wakes are held over two days, and each evening a supper is served to the family, neighbors and close friends—sometimes 100 to 200 or more will be fed. And about 7 p.m. each evening, a long string of buggies begins to pull into the newly made parking lots as the young single people in the community assemble to sing hymns to the family. The young singers can number from a couple hundred to 500 or 600, selecting songs from hymn books as they go. When finished, about an hour later, they pay their respects to the deceased by filing silently past the coffin, and the other mourners file past for a final viewing as well.

On the third day, the funeral services often begin at 9 a.m. If the body had been in the house for viewing, the pallbearers will have carried the coffin to the tent for the funeral service, placed near where the family members are sitting in the center of the tent.

Close relatives, extended family and close friends will fill the tent, and if more room is needed mourners can sit on benches in the house. Most of the rooms would have been emptied of the beds, couches and other furniture to accommodate the crowd. If there's 1,000 or more, a shed will likely be used for the overflow, too. That means there will be preachers in the tent, shed and house, each preaching their own sermons. A funeral service typically has four ministers in each location— the first presents a 30-minute sermon, the second preaches for about 45 minutes, the third reads the obituary and makes a few comments, and the fourth preaches for 10 to 15 minutes.

"The coming together before the funeral … you'd probably be amazed at how many people come. It's friends from all over the community." –Bishop

The sermons are preached in the standard German, and the sermons are not necessarily about the dead, though they might be mentioned. The sermons are conducted foremost to remind the mourners that death will greet each one of them, and it can come within the twinkling of an eye, and they must be ready and prepared to face the Lord. The sermons are not passive, but aggressively preached, sometimes with shouting, as the ministers implore the mourners to search their souls to make sure they are preparing for Judgment Day.

The first sermon is often from the book of Genesis and reminds mourners of Adam and Eve's transgressions and eviction from the Garden. The second is typically about salvation and resurrection. The other is about the importance of prayer and of asking for forgiveness and courage and guidance.

Children of all ages are included at the funerals. If several children in an Amish parochial school know the deceased, the school might close for the day. And because the Amish parents do not use babysitters, even infants are brought along

89

to the wakes and funerals. It's common for mothers to sit on the wooden bench through the two-hour long funeral service with an infant on her lap or shoulder and a few preschoolers beside her. When pacifiers don't keep crying infants satisfied, the mothers take the babies outside. The other church members are tolerant and patient and the ministers preach over the crying. Midway through the service, a selection of treats like graham crackers and pretzels are passed to the children.

All the women and girls wear black dresses and black capes or aprons for the funerals, along with their white head coverings. The men and boys are also in black, trousers and jackets or vests, with white shirts. The men wear black broad-brimmed felt or straw hats.

When all the sermons and prayers have been said, the pallbearers release the rows of mourners one at a time to file out and view the body. Then the close family gathers around the coffin and allows themselves another look at their loved one before the lid is placed atop the coffin. The pallbearers put on their hats and carry the coffin to Obadiah Helmuth's buggy for the trip to the cemetery.

The funeral procession of buggies and a few vehicles leaves for the cemetery while neighbor women stay behind to prepare the meal. Men who stay behind stack the wooden benches in the tent into tables.

At the cemetery, the pallbearers have already dug the grave by hand. Two mounds of dirt remain on each side of the open grave. Finished sawhorses are set up a distance away from the grave and when the coffin and family arrive, the pallbearers place the body on the sawhorses.

The top half of the lid is opened and mourners file by once again. The immediate family is the last to view the deceased, and they take their time in the still and quiet of the country cemetery for their last moments on earth with their loved one. Then one of the pallbearers slowly and gently closes the coffin lid. The pallbearers carry it to the grave and with heavy straps lower it into a rough pine box in the open grave. They lower a lid onto it and place another layer of pine planks on top.

ARTICLE 18 FROM THE
DORDRECHT CONFESSION OF FAITH

A DOCUMENT THAT DATES BACK TO 1632 AND IS USED TO INSTRUCT CANDIDATES FOR BAPTISM

Concerning the resurrection of the dead, we confess with the mouth and believe the same with the heart that according to Scripture all men who have died and fallen asleep shall again be awakened, made alive, and raised up the last day by the incomprehensible power of God. These together with those who will then remain alive shall be changed in the twinkling of an eye at the sound of the last trumpet and be placed before the judgment seat of Christ, where the good shall be separated from the wicked, and then each one shall receive in his own body according to what he has done, whether it be good or evil.

And that the good or pious, as the blessed, shall then be taken up to be with Christ to enter into eternal life and obtain that joy which no one has seen nor no ear has heard nor has entered into any man's heart. And that they shall reign and triumph with Christ from everlasting to everlasting.

The minister offers prayers and reads a hymn such as, "Now we bring the body to rest and cover it with earth . . ." As a small chorus of Amish men and women sing, the pallbearers begin to fill the grave, one shovelful at a time. Some grandchildren or other relatives also step in to help with the filling of the grave. No one leaves or moves or speaks until the grave is filled and the sod is replaced over the grave.

The mourners return to their buggies for the ride back to the deceased's home for the dinner.

Since the funeral begins at 9 a.m. and most begin arriving by 8, it can be a long day. All of the above can last until 2 or 2:30 p.m. And for those who stay for dinner the day will last until 4 or 5. But this is time the Amish are willing to give to their grieving family and friends. There are few if any variations in the funeral tradition. The funerals are all done the same way, following the same template that's been used for these

"We believe in ashes to ashes, dust to dust." –Obadiah Helmuth

home funerals for generations. No one decides to hold private graveside services. No one decides to use a funeral home rather than have services at home. No one decides not to serve meals. No one decides to use a hearse to take the coffin to the cemetery instead of a buggy.

The day after the funeral, neighbors will help with the return of dishes and pans and other cleanup. No one asks or tells them how to do what they do; they've been going to funerals since they were born and know what needs to be done. They know how to neighbor.

Some can quote the chapter and verse that talks about loving your neighbor. Some can recite lines from hymns about being good neighbors. And some simply say, it's what's expected.

"It's all part of our lifestyle," said a bishop. "If someone needs help, we try to help, and not so we can get help in return if we ever need it. We want to help out of love for our fellow man. When we grew up, this was practiced in the home and we learned it without being told. And we do it because that's just what you do."

The local coffinmaker, Obadiah Helmuth, has specially fitted a buggy so he can carry the coffins from the home to the cemeteries.

The Amish bury their dead in simple coffins, and as with everything Amish, they're all alike. There are no frills and no options to be fancier than another. They are stained and varnished poplar boxes lined with plain white muslin. Sometimes, excelsior or shredded newspaper is used to put a little padding between the muslin and the box. An adult-sized coffin costs around $300.

Obadiah Helmuth, 79, who lives south of Arthur, has been making coffins since he was 18 years old.

The workshop behind his house holds a few coffins he's been working on. In a side room, dark and kind of eerie, Oba keeps finished coffins on racks.

Often, he makes one when he gets the news of a death. If he starts in the morning he has it finished by evening.

"This here, I can pert' near do with my eyes closed," he said.

He said he builds coffins, not caskets. A casket has straight sides, he explained, but the sides of the coffin are wider near the waist and taper toward the feet.

The Amish don't use concrete vaults. Instead, the coffin is placed in a simple pine "rough box."

"We believe in ashes to ashes, dust to dust," Oba said.

Amish women are usually buried in their dark Sunday dresses with their capes and apron. The men are buried in white shirts and a dark suit.

The lid of the coffin is removed for viewing the body, which lies in state in the deceased's own home, or that of a relative.

Oba said after death the bodies are taken to a funeral home for embalming. Burial often occurs the third day after death. The pallbearers dig the grave.

A death in the Amish community draws large numbers of people, and a wake typically is held over two days. An Amish funeral can draw 500 to 5,000.

There are no funeral bouquets on the coffin or at the home or at an Amish cemetery.

"That's just something we don't do," he said. "We try to keep it all simple."

Oba takes the coffin to the cemetery in a special buggy, which has had the back seat removed so the coffin can slide underneath the driver's seat. The family follows in buggies lined up in descending order from the oldest to the youngest child.

At the cemetery, there are more prayers and another viewing of the body. The four pallbearers (sometimes six) lower the coffin into the ground and fill the grave with dirt while hymns are sung.

Then the mourners return to the deceased's home for a light meal, provided by friends and relatives. With the help of the church wagons, there are benches enough to make tables. Oba recalls one recent funeral that drew about 650 people. He remembers they had 80 quarts of noodles, 12 casseroles, 66 quarts of rice, 17 trays of 48 sandwiches each, pudding, salads, cakes, pies and fruit.

Obadiah and his wife, Anna Mae, have 12 children. In all his years of making coffins, he's never had a problem dealing with a family.

"It's a time when they're broken-hearted," he said. "And yeah, there's times when you just cry with them."

'Standardbred for sale: Amish born and broke'

*The Amish often get their
Standardbred horses
off the racetrack.
Standardbreds are trotting
horses most commonly used in
harness racing.*

H oward Chupp has a large workshop for buggy-making alongside Springfield Road, about as far east as one can get in the Amish settlement in Douglas County.

His home and farm with the big barn and rolling pastures sits behind his workshop. Like most Amish men who have their own business, Howard gave up working for an employer—in his case the Horizon hardware store—to start his own home-based shop. He wanted to be near home to help raise his two sons and three daughters. He's one of three in the community to make traditional Amish buggies; he also makes carts and open buggies for non-Amish customers.

Howard opened his shop in 1997 when his boys were 10 and 11. Now, Daniel and Marlin are 21 and 22 and they work alongside him in the shop.

That kind of family business is common in the Amish community, as fathers and sons work in trades that do everything from barn building to cabinet-making to roofing, plumbing and more.

The three men can build a buggy from the ground up in 80 to 90 hours, Howard said. The wood frame is 3/4-inch plywood that's primed, sanded and painted and the exterior covering is black vinyl. They also build the interior seats and upholster in vinyl or plush velvetlike material.

With proper care, a buggy can last 20 years or more. He said most Amish families will order a new buggy for their son when he is between the ages of 16 and 21. Some will buy a buggy for their daughters, too.

Howard, an outgoing man with a big voice, said that although Daniel and Marlin make buggies all day long, they don't have their own.

"They're still using Dad's!" he said.

According to an Amish farmer, buggies go about 10 to 12 mph, so if you see one going 15 mph, it's probably a teenage driver. Howard laughed but said it's not always true.

"We have a fella close to 70 who goes through here probably going 15 mph," he said. "He drives different horses, but if he's got a good horse, he's going pretty fast. And my father-in-law's in his 60s and he doesn't like to drive a plug either.

"And I don't either," he said.

The plywood frames might not seem like they'd afford much protection sharing the roads with semis and SUVs, but Howard said the Amish people grow up in buggies and feel safe and comfortable and there aren't a lot of buggy accidents. He said sometimes when a buggy gets banged up it's not from a car or truck.

"Sometimes they'll have a horse that can get his hind legs up and kick out the windshield. Or sometimes there's runaways. A horse that runs off. That happens."

BUGGIES IN DETAIL

Frame:	Wooden, 3/4-inch plywood
Seats:	Most often four, sometimes six
Life expectancy:	20 years or more with proper care
Cost:	$4,000 to $6,000
Weight:	800 pounds
Maintenance:	Occasional washing with Murphy's Oil Soap
Color:	Black in the Arthur-Arcola community
Interior:	Buyer's choice. Most seats are covered in velvet-like upholstery or vinyl. Blue and gray are popular colors.
State requirements:	Headlights, rear lights, reflective triangle on back and rear amber flashers
Horsepower:	Usually a Standardbred
Distance covered:	With a good horse, 20 miles can be covered in two hours. And a good horse can make the return trip the same day.
Speed:	10 to 12 mph
Heat:	Small propane heater; some buggies are not heated and passengers use a heavy robe to keep warm.
Lights:	Battery powered
Windshield wipers:	Manual
Buggies per family:	In most Amish homes, the husband and wife each have their own buggy.
Harness and hitch:	5 minutes.

But in February 2007, a heavy morning fog, a slow-moving horse and buggy and an SUV all contributed to a fatal accident north of Arthur.

Willis A. Miller, 52, of rural Arthur, died from injuries he received when the horse and buggy he was driving on the Atwood-Arthur Road was hit from behind by a SUV driven by a 28-year-old Atwood man.

The driver told police he didn't see the buggy in the heavy fog.

A very few of the roads in the Amish community in Moultrie and Douglas counties have buggy lanes. The Illinois Department of Transportation is talking about widening Springfield Road and adding buggy lanes, as well as adding buggy lanes to the Atwood-Arthur Road.

The Amish would like to have them.

Douglas County Sheriff's Sgt. Craig Patton estimated his office receives between five and 10 accident reports a year that involve buggies. Moultrie County Sheriff Jeff Thomas said his office receives "a few."

"Most of the crashes that occur are usually from people not familiar with the area," Thomas said. "Most everybody else is used to Amish buggies and how slow they go and accommodate them very well."

"A horse and buggy's safer (in ice and snow) than a van. The horse shoes have diamond chunks in a bronze alloy on the bottom and that horse is not going to slip. He can go anywhere." –Howard Chupp

"Sometimes they'll have a horse that can get his hind legs up and kick out the windshield. Or sometimes there's runaways. A horse that runs off. That happens." –Howard Chupp

95

Used buggies

It never fails to catch the eye. Driving down Illinois 133 between Arthur and Arcola one passes by the small burg of Chesterville, which can claim a popular family-owned restaurant, the Dutch Valley Meats processing plant and—a used Amish buggy lot.

Yep, right there next to a cluster of buildings offering custom-made poker chips and Beanie Babies is the green-and-white striped canopy that shades a collection of used Amish buggies, open-air carriages and buckboard wagons.

Owner Paul Schrock accidentally got into used buggy sales three or four years ago, when an Amish man who repaired buggies decided to get out of the business. Schrock bought six used buggies, put them outside his shop alongside the highway, and "Bam, bam, bam! They were gone," said Schrock's daughter, Michelle.

But not to Amish families, who buy used buggies at farm sales or auctions.

The buyers come from all over the country after seeing Schrock's Web site or finding the buggies on eBay. Some want them to use with their own horses for pleasure and some want the sleighs and wagons for lawn decorations, he said.

Recently, he offered a closed-in double-seat Amish buggy ($995); an open pony buggy ($795); an antique Christmas sleigh ($995); an antique doctor's buggy "fixer upper—needs work" ($595); an open carriage with surrey fringed top ($2,450); a pony-sized buckboard wagon ($1,995) and several others, including a pony-sized stagecoach ($1,995).

The most expensive one currently on the lot is a fancy open carriage with surrey top, "new condition" for $3,995—on sale.

Schrock calls his business My Amish Heritage because he grew up in an Amish home until the age of 7 or 8, when his family left that faith to join the Mennonite church. He has common relatives among the Amish in the area, the largest settlement of Amish in the state.

The Schrocks have shipped their "kind, gently used buggies" all over the country.

"And last year at Christmas, we sold six or eight antique sleighs," Michelle said. "Two of them went into Canada to a movie prop company there."

"We had one on dipslay here at our store and sold it on eBay. We sell most of them on our Web site." –Michelle Schrock

'… in your conduct be friendly toward everyone …'

–from Rules of a Godly Life

They're called snowbirds; northerners who fly south for the winter. But on the outskirts of Sarasota, Fla., in a little community called Pinecraft, they're called Amish Snowbirds. More than a thousand, maybe as many as 2,000 to 3,000, Amish and their close religious kin, the Mennonites, escape the dangerous ice and snow to bask in the 70-degree temperatures in rented bungalows along palm-lined streets.

No horses and buggies here. As one drives to the outskirts of Sarasota on a four-lane highway called Bahia Vista, there's an abundance of adult-sized tricycles being ridden on the sidewalks.

On the narrow side streets with names like Graber, Kruppa or Schrock, even more tricycles are being pedaled about by the people dressed in plain dark clothing, men with beards as white as the snow they've escaped, the women with their prayer

Many of the winter residents staying at Pinecraft post signs out in front of their rental apartments and bungalows stating their hometowns and states.

caps and dark stockings. They frequently stop and visit, catching up, creating new friendships, talking most often in their common language of Pennsylvania Dutch, inquiring about a common relative or acquaintance.

"Don't come to Pinecraft if you don't like to socialize," cracked an Amish bishop from Holmes County, Ohio. He and a minister from Connieville, Pa., had stopped in Big Olaf's ice cream shop to visit with another Amish man, also a minister, working behind the counter.

"Some people come for a week, some three months, and some will go back and forth." –Ella Toy

The big event of the day, the three advised, happens at noon behind the Mennonite Tourist Church. Can't miss it, they chuckled. That's when the bus arrives. As many as 75 to 100 people will go down on those days to see who gets off the bus. As many as six or seven luxury coaches serving the Amish communities in Pennsylvania, Delaware, Ohio, Wisconsin, Indiana, Iowa, Michigan, Missouri and of course, Illinois, bring new arrivals down each week. In a few days, the buses will return with the folks destined to return, ready or not, to the weather back home. It's about a 19-hour trip to Arthur. When enough of them are signed up, the bus picks them up in front of Melvin Otto's canvas shop on Illinois 133. When there are only a few, the bus company sends a van to take them to Seymour, Ind. There, they can board the bus coming down from the Amish settlements in northern Indiana.

"There isn't any place in the world like Pinecraft," said the Holmes County minister.

He had come down for a 12-day visit to get warm, he said. Amish folks don't get to travel much to visit family and friends in other states, he said, so the thrill of Pinecraft is as a meeting-up place. Some families separated by distance arrange to come down at the same time; many delight in the daily surprises of running across a second-cousin or an aunt and uncle they haven't seen for years.

It's a home away from home, says Freeman Beachy of Arthur. "And it just keeps growing," he said, noting that the former "boundaries" now extend out into other subdivisions. "Oh, it's really spread out."

There is a small winter haven for the Amish near Phoenix, where about 40-some attend church, he said. Pinecraft, on the other hand, is the largest coming-together spot for the Amish and Mennonites in the world. It's their own small town. It has shops within walking distance, bike rentals and a fabric store with goods for Amish dresses and quilts.

The Amish people can go anywhere they want to escape the cold, but an Amish family by itself on the beach at Fort Lauderdale would draw stares. It's more comfortable being with others of the same faith and values. And most importantly, in their own small town, they can have church.

The 60 or so families who have permanent homes at Pinecraft have a church meeting place in a former bakery building, and now there is another building they call the "extension" for the temporary residents in the winter time. That former home can accommodate about 500 within earshot of the minister with benches in the large main room, foyer, quilt house and paved area outside.

One Sunday in mid-February, Beachy said there were at least 500 at the extension church, nearly 300 at the permanent church house and some Amish even attended the Mennonite Tourist Church, which he heard was packed.

In Pinecraft's extension church, there is a large open room with wooden benches. The first few rows have chairs for the older men and women; some tape their names on the chairs to reserve their spots.

As in all Amish church services, the men sit at the front of the room, the oldest ones in the first rows. Because the number of winter residents in Pinecraft is increasing, there's been talk about the need for a larger meeting house for church services.

But Beachy said since the county would look at it as a "church," officials would require a parking lot with X-number of parking spots.

"We walk or take our bikes," Beachy said. "And for us it's really not a church house. It's a meeting place. So what we're encouraging, if (Pinecraft) keeps growing, which it looks like it will, is to have a third home someplace for a third smaller group, rather than two large groups. That's what we do at home. If our (church) district gets too big we'll geographically divide up and form a new district. That can be done here."

Who gets to preach is determined by the local bishop, who keeps track of the visiting ministers, their years of experience and the last time they preached in Pinecraft.

And though the Amish come from all over the country, they know the same hymns and melodies, sung without benefit of a piano.

"It's the newlyweds and the half-deads," –Amish woman visiting Pinecraft, Fla.

"Each state might have a little variation, a little different twist in the hymn, but it's surprising how well we can all sing together," Beachy said. "But if there's a lot of Pennsylvania men sitting close together, everything's practically the same but Pennsylvania's a little bit different—we say they have more hills. They go up and down, up and down," he joked.

Freeman Beachy first saw Pinecraft as a teenager in the '50s. He and his wife, Bertha, took occasional vacations there and then about 12 years ago they built a small spec home. Bertha liked it so well they decided to keep it, and now spend five months a year there.

They arrive in mid-November—she helps make pies at Yoder's Kitchen for the Thanksgiving rush. Pie-hungry Sarasota residents buy 3,000-plus pies at Yoder's Kitchen for the holiday. Freeman Beachy said he helps out there beginning three days before Thanksgiving, helping people carry pies to their cars. Some people buy six or seven pies.

"It's a circus," he laughed.

The Beachys also help their people find rentals in Pinecraft. The bungalows and the small rental units offer the bare essentials. They rent in the neighborhood of $30 to $40 a day.

David Schrock of Arthur jokes that in their rental unit, their bedroom is in the living room, which is in the kitchen. It's comfortable and meets their needs for the two months the Shrocks are able to get away. They cook most of their own meals, and even bring down a box of their own canned goods.

Some snowbirds stay only a week or so. And young families sometimes arrive with little children to visit the grandmas and grandpas.

Since so many Amish men now work in Amish-owned woodshops that close the last week of December, many vacation in Pinecraft and stay with relatives.

"It is really packed around here the week between Christmas and New Year's," said Ella Toy at Alma Sue's Quilt Shop.

A few miles from Pinecraft, the hotel clerk's face brightens when asked directions to Pinecraft.

"Ah! Pinecraft—That's where the Aimish live," he said, pronouncing Amish with a hard A. "They have great restaurants there; the Dutch Heritage seats 650. It's the largest one in town."

The three restaurants in Pinecraft certainly draw the crowds.

A short ride up the block from the heart of Pinecraft is Troyer's Dutch Heritage restaurant, the one that seats 650. It also has a store with baked goods, like iced cinnamon rolls, jams and jellies and apple butter, a large refrigerated case with cheeses and an expansive gift shop with Vera Bradley purses and sequined T-shirts, staffed by Amish girls, but not intended for Amish customers.

The bike racks outside overflow in the morning as Amish men show up at Troyer's for coffee and talk.

In the winter season, the restaurant partitions off a portion of its dining room for the coffee shop, which draws 100 or more. Its large breakfast buffet offers tomato gravy, a uniquely Amish favorite for saucing up scrambled eggs and hash browns.

Mom's Country Cafe also tempts customers with its Amish cooking and a glass case filled with pies. Nearby is Olaf's ice cream shop, which also features Amish cheeses, jams and jellies. The area also has two large Amish furniture stores and a cabinet shop featuring the handiwork of Amish woodworkers from up north.

Alma Sue's Quilt Shop is also on the busy street. Five Amish and Mennonite women were working at a quilting frame, deftly quilting the top of a bedspread. All but one of the five women were widows. Normally they are paid by the shop owner to quilt, but that day they were working without charge because the quilt would be raffled for a Mennonite charity.

"There were 20 widows sitting around the table at (breakfast) this morning," one said, making the point that there are more women than men in Pinecraft. But there are young people too.

"It's the newlyweds and the half-deads," cracked an Amish woman from Holmes County, Ohio.

Coach

The Amish from Arthur who make the trip south to the winter haven called Pinecraft, Fla., get there on the convenience of a luxury coach line.

C&C Coach Xpress out of Pierceton in northern Indiana began serving the Arthur community three years ago.

"We come to Arthur every other week, lately every week," said C&C owner Jo Clevenger, who also serves Amish in Nappanee, Goshen, Shipshewana, Topeka, Fort Wayne and other Indiana communities.

It's affordable, with fares for seniors running about $220 a couple, one way. And she said the riders do seem to have fun.

"Of course, we do not play the TV," she said. "But it's a nice group. They're always very polite. The little kids are well-behaved. And they sing (hymns) a lot.

"I can't really ask for better travelers."

Driver Belinda Pruitt said she enjoys the Amish because they like to tell jokes, and occasionally a man will stand up and share a joke over the bus microphone.

"Of course, they all speak the Dutch," she said, "but if you ask them what they're talking about, they'll tell you."

She's always amazed when she reaches Pinecraft and pulls into the parking lot behind the Mennonite Church.

"I've seen as many as 250 waiting there, to see who's getting off the bus. Of course, some have family they're waiting for, but others are just there to see who's coming in," Pruitt said.

Also, young single folks come down to live for a few months. They'll share apartments with friends, Freeman Beachy said. The boys work as bricklayers or carpenters, while the girls get jobs in the restaurants. In the evenings, the young gather in the park to play volleyball and basketball.

"The young people who come down here come for the social life," said Ella Toy, who owns Alma Sue's. "It's a great place for them to meet new people from other communities."

Toy, a Mennonite, pays Amish women to quilt for her in their homes. But there is a lot of quilting going on in Pinecraft just for fun.

Many bring their quilt-tops and fabric from home; some bring their own portable sewing machines.

The "extension" that holds the church service is one of the places where women gather around quilting frames. As many as 10 women may show up to work on that day's project. There's no sign-up sheet, no assignments. They join in when they can. They keep their threaded needles, ready for action, thread premeasured, stuck into the bottom of empty Styrofoam egg cartons on top of the quilt. They visit over their work and might finish a couple quilts in a week.

On the other side of Pinecraft, the men shuffle.

Shuffleboard is so popular in Pinecraft that the park has eight shuffleboard courts and scores of men arrive as soon as the boards are dry enough in the morning.

"It's a busy place," Freeman Beachy said. "They get a crowd over there and it goes all the way up 'til it gets dark."

Frequently, the snowbirds from each state meet in the covered pavilion for a state reunion. One night recently, 1,100 Amish and Mennonites showed up for a barbecue chicken dinner, a fund-raiser to go toward paying for the expansion of the pavilion.

And a lot of visiting goes on.

"Come in, come in," says Dan Hochstetler. The 90-year-old from Topeka, Ind., calls to knocks on his apartment door. He welcomes them in.

"This is Katie," he says, introducing his 88-year-old wife. "She's the only wife I ever had and she's the best wife I ever had."

The Hochstetlers are among some of the most beloved snow-

"There isn't any place in the world like Pinecraft." –Amish minister from Holmes County, Ohio

birds in Pinecraft, and there is a steady stream of visitors at the door to their small apartment, evident by the number of bicycles and tricycles that come and go. The couple keeps a semicircle of chairs in their kitchen-living area to visit with callers. A spiral notebook that their guests sign holds thousands of names and addresses.

To an outsider, it seems clear the most enjoyable aspect of living in Pinecraft is the visiting. Since the Amish aren't preoccupied with demands on time like watching CSI or American Idol or surfing the Internet, they have the time to visit—the old-fashioned way. They knock on a door, sit down and talk. They do it in their home communities, but since they don't have to go hitch a horse to a buggy and travel down a road, it's easier in Pinecraft. And they do it all day and all evening long.

The Hochstetlers have been wintering in Pinecraft for 25 years, and guests are always welcome. Dan remembers the days when Pinecraft's streets were gravel, and the busy four-lane Bahia street was a two-lane highway.

"There's a lot more people now. Used to say there were 500 apartments to rent; I don't know what it is now, but more than that!"

He writes history articles for an Amish publication called The Connection. She's a scribe for The Budget, the Amish national newspaper. One of their daughters and her husband are down visiting. There's talk among all about the deep snow and cold temperatures at home.

He notes he still has a buggy back on his farm—but the kids took his horse away.

The horse got too frisky, Dan said, and they said he didn't have any business being out on the road in a buggy.

In Pinecraft, both Dan and Katie have tricycles.

If anyone needs to go a farther distance, a city bus runs right by. It's 50 cents for a ride downtown—25 cents for seniors.

Beachy said the transit system is adding more buses to the schedule to accommodate the Amish visitors. Schrock rides the bus with his fishing pole and tackle box to fish in the Sarasota Bay.

The Amish live with electricity while in Pinecraft, and even if they chose to forego it, city restrictions wouldn't allow it, Beachy said. But the Amish are often mistakenly thought to believe that there is something inherently evil or bad about electricity, and they don't. In fact, in their own homes they use batteries and compressors to run power equipment when needed. What they have against electricity in the home is the temptations it brings with it—televisions, radios, stereos, computers and all the other trappings of modern living.

The Amish keep their lives simple and uncluttered so they can focus on their faith and families. They use horses and buggies because it limits their daily comings and goings outside their rural community.

In Pinecraft, they use electric lamps, but there are no televisions or radios or computers. Some use electric washers and dryers provided in the apartments, and many use the washers but still prefer to hang clothes outside to dry.

"It's like staying in a hotel room," Beachy said. "We use (electricity) because it's there. But when we get back home we get back to the gas lamps and don't even really think about it."

In the quiet of their little apartments they write letters home, sew and just like at home, read the Bible. They make time for their devotions.

The popularity among the Amish is driving the price of land up in the Pinecraft area. Beachy said prices are higher in Pinecraft than across the Phillipi River in the city of Sarasota.

And there's no room to expand. The housing is pretty tight now, with the bungalows on very small lots; some garages have been converted into rental units, too.

If a couple wants to winter in Pinecraft next year, they'd better reserve a spot now.

"Some say, why don't you just go out east of town and start a new Pinecraft? But nobody wants to go," Beachy said. "They want to stay in Pinecraft."

'… gladly share the bounties you receive …'

–from Rules of a Godly Life

On Friday evenings in January and February 2007, a 15-passenger van left Arthur carrying groups of young Amish men south to Florida. Not for a sunny vacation, but to repair hurricane-damaged homes.

This is the third year the volunteers spent a week or more repairing homes damaged in 2005 by Hurricane Wilma in the Florida communities of Arcadia, Wachula and Immokalee.

Monroe Herschberger, a 66-year-old Amish carpenter from rural Sullivan, came up with the idea to create Arthur Disaster Services. He became inspired to help people in need, he said, after studying the Book of Matthew 25:35-40.

"In the commentary it tells you that we should not depend on intelligence, wealth or knowledge, and we can't look to the government or the churches to take care of the needy," Herschberger said. "It takes our own personal help."

And Herschberger said that with so much destruction from the hurricanes in Mississippi, Louisiana and Florida, people often wondered if God was trying to send a message. Herschberger said he asked himself if the disasters could be a test of faith, to see if one has the compassion to help those in need.

After giving his plan some serious thought, he announced his intentions at church. No one talked him out of it, so he sought pledges from two Amish-owned businesses. He walked away with $5,000 to get the volunteers transportation and lodging. Another business threw in $3,500.

"It was outstanding. It was just overwhelming," Herschberger said of the response.

The first year, 88 young men signed up to work in Florida, and this year he had close to 200. Last year, they rebuilt 13 homes in Wachula.

This winter in Immokalee, they made repairs to about 100 homes, said Rick Heers, minister of the Friendship Baptist Church, which purchases the building materials for Herschberger's workers.

Heers raves about the Amish men who came to work in Immokalee.

"Oh my goodness, my goodness," Heers said. "They're wonderful. They're extremely helpful. In fact, I've been trying to get in touch with Monroe so we can get him back here. We've got about 200 more homes that need to be rehabbed.

"We have been so impressed with their workmanship. Their work is superb."

Herschberger said Arthur's Amish church districts have donated the money to cover the transportation costs and food. Herschberger's wife, Mary, is the chief cook, and she also brings along a few young Amish women to help with meals, as well as the cleaning and laundry. All sleep in a day-care center in the basement of the Friendship Baptist Church.

One of the young women, Ruby Stutzman of Arthur, spent two weeks helping Mary. She liked the experience and might go back next year.

"It's a chance to help people get a new house," Stutzman said. "And they need a lot of help down there."

Margaret Plank, 21, of Arthur said she considered the volunteer work a chance to serve God.

Volunteer Jason Duitsman, 24, of Arthur said he didn't mind spending a week doing repairs.

"We're supposed to help when people are in need, and that's a good place to do that," Duitsman said.

And Clifford Schrock, 19, said it's not all hard labor: "It's a lot of fun being with friends and also helping someone in need."

Monroe Herschberger said it's been an eye opener for the young people to see the poverty in those central Florida towns. Immokalee has a diverse population with many immigrants from Cuba and Mexico as well as Native Americans. Some of their living conditions are shocking, he said, and even though the hurricanes damaged their homes almost three years ago, many still have blue tarps over roofs and broken windows that haven't been replaced.

"(At first, we got) a treatment like 'Who are these creatures?' Ya know, we are dressed different. They wouldn't hardly talk to us. But after we were there like three weeks, after they found out what we were doing, a lot of people there were as happy as could be." –Monroe Herschberger

"When I first went down there, I couldn't believe what I saw," Herschberger said. "And I tell the kids if you want to become instantly rich, you just go to these places, and you'll realize how much you have."

It takes a lot of patience to oversee the mission work, and Herschberger said he is often frustrated dealing with the red tape of the cities and counties. At times, he has workers on hand ready to work, but the supplies and materials have not been purchased.

Herschberger is known as a go-getter to folks in Arthur, said Freeman Beachy, a longtime friend.

"I'm amazed with the energy he still has to pursue this and the responsibility that goes with it," Beachy said. "But we think it's good for our young folks to have those experiences, to go out and help other people. It makes us appreciate the life and opportunity that we have and the home life that we have."

Though the mission work originated in Arthur, volunteers from Amish communities in Michigan and Indiana are also getting involved. Some Amish communities in Ohio are talking about starting their own service mission.

Beachy said he remembers the years when their Amish forefathers seemed to focus on helping those who lived within the Amish community.

"Today we're reaching out farther and farther all the time," Beachy said.

Herschberger said the work of the Amish volunteers over the last three years amounts to a "drop in a five-gallon bucket," considering all the homes that remain untouched.

He encourages those who would like to support the work to send donations to Arthur Disaster Services, Route 1, Box 214, Sullivan, IL 61951. He said the mission has no operating or overhead expenses, so virtually all donations go to the cause.

Heers said there are no Amish in central Florida, so most of the people of Immokalee didn't know what to think of the young men with their suspenders and homemade denim breeches and plain cotton shirts.

"They'd see them around town and they'd see them hanging their clothes to dry out on the line," Heers said, and some might have thought they were different or odd.

But as soon as they saw how expert they were at the repairs, the residents had no trouble warming up to the Amish men. They became friends with many.

"The young men are very nice. Very gentle men," Heers said. "They're very helpful and they listen to (Monroe) and are careful to follow his instructions. It's nice to watch him and see the way he teaches them.

"They're thoughtful and kind and generous. We've sat in their place and had them sing hymns to us, and we sang to them. We were like one."

Afterword

It doesn't seem right that one of the saddest days in a person's life should be spent under a bright, hazy sky. But there it was, a glorious backdrop to a painful day as I stood at the side of the grave of a good friend, saying goodbye.

If he'd have been there, and I could have explained what I felt, I'm sure that David D. Schrock, an Amish minister and farmer, would have said he had spent most of his 67 years preparing for his final journey to meet the Lord. He would have appreciated the light breeze that day and liked that his wife, Lizzie Ann, three children and 14 grandchildren would not have had rain or lightning added to their troubles.

I know he wasn't ready to leave his family, but I feel sure he anticipated being with them again. I feel certain he would have found the bright sky to his liking.

I watched his family at the cemetery as they viewed his body one last time, and as they stood at the grave and silently watched as four pallbearers put a shovelful of dirt — one shovelful at a time — atop the rough box holding his coffin.

The clods of dirt hit the box with a soft, gentle thud but there was no other sound in the air. No train whistles, no crying crows, no airplanes flying overhead, just the ominous silence of grief. All seemed frozen, watching sadly as the grave filled. Then the strips of sod were laid atop the grave. And it was over. The earthly life of David D. Schrock had come to an end.

A year earlier almost to the day of his death on Oct. 6, 2007, I'd been standing with him in that same cemetery. I had talked with him while he painted the tombstones of his parents and ancestors. That day, too, was a beautiful, breezy day. I remember asking him why there were no flowers at the cemetery. Not even a planted mum poked through the soil near a stone. He answered by singing a little tune: "Give me the roses while I live, trying to cheer me on. Useless the flowers that you give, after the soul is gone."

I learned a lot from him through the nearly 20 years I knew him. I'd asked him hundreds of questions, and also had the privilege of chatting with him about things not related to being Amish, like comfortable shoes, applesauce recipes and of course, each of our grandchildren. I could say plenty of complimentary things about him. But I know he would discourage it. "Praise is for the Lord," he would say, "not man."

Through the years, I'd heard several in the Amish community call him gifted. His preaching was said to be some of the most inspiring, and he frequently was asked to give the sermon at funerals. At his wake, one Amish man told me he'd heard what turned out to be David's last sermon. The man said when he and his wife left, he turned to her and said, "That was something special." When he learned of David's death, he realized why.

As news of David's passing circulated through the Amish neighborhoods the weekend of Oct. 6, I heard many react by saying his death would leave a big hole in the community. His funeral and wake drew thousands—and thousands—throughout the days and evenings from Sunday through the burial on Tuesday. Some estimated more than 200 ministers arrived at the home place southeast of Arthur, and Amish taxi-vans parked at the home had license plates from Ohio, Indiana, Iowa, Kansas, Kentucky and other states. The crowd for the funeral was so large it filled a huge tent, all the first floor of the farmhouse and David's and Lizzie's little house and a large shed. Twelve ministers gave the sermons. Some neighbors estimated 800 meals were served after the funeral at the house.

And though 99 percent of those who came to pay their last respects were dressed in the black and white of the Amish, several in the crowd were non-Amish. David tolerated outsiders better than most and was frequently the one that Amish people pointed the inquisitive to for answers and guidance. I was one. He made genuine friends with many of us.

I heard at the wake from an acquaintance that when David preached at funerals when non-Amish were in the crowd, he'd often stop speaking in the standard German to explain the gist of it in English. David decided if he was going to be preaching the words of Jesus, the non-Amish person might need to hear that more than anybody else that day, and he continued the practice.

Some 20 years ago, when I knocked for the first time on the door of his farmhouse, I seem to remember David opened the door with a toothpick still in the corner of his mouth. He'd just finished lunch. I babbled off in a long roundabout way, telling him I wanted to do some stories about the Amish for The News-Gazette. He invited me into his living room where we talked while Lizzie Ann cleaned up the dishes after dinner. I remember telling him I was a farmer's daughter, that I'd once raised my own pig, that my dad raised bees—dredging up anything and everything I could think of that might warm him up and help him decide to help me with the story.

Since then I've stopped by David's and Lizzie's house a couple of hundred times. I stayed in touch with David and Lizzie through the years and learned in 1990 that a sore throat led him to see a doctor who discovered non-Hodgkin's lymphoma. After the cancer went into remission, he struggled with a weakened heart. Unable to farm any longer, he turned over the farming to his son, Howard.

I stopped by to visit them in 2005, and it had been several years since we talked. When he answered the door I might not have recognized him if I'd met him on the street. Lizzie seemed to never change, and we picked up our conversations like we'd never stopped talking. But David's cancer and heart condition had seemed to shrink him in stature. His voice even seemed a little weaker, though his laugh and sharp sense of humor remained unscathed.

Over the past year, I rarely stopped at David and Lizzie's when at least one of the grandchildren next door wouldn't wander in to see who was visiting. I remember sitting out in their front yard one summer evening to catch a cool breeze, talking to David and Lizzie, and the two littlest girls came up and started having a delightful conversation with me in Dutch. I remember they crawled over his legs and up on his lap, while his older grandchildren got ready to have a water fight. He reminded me that up the road were his other seven grandchildren. He and Lizzie had their son and two daughters and all their grandchildren within

arm's reach. Life didn't get much better than that, he said. He had all he needed.

When I first told him we wanted to do this project, he didn't respond for quite a while. Finally, he explained he couldn't stop me, but he didn't want to have an active part in it. He'd give me names of other Amish ministers and bishops that could help me get it right, but I needed to get my information from other people, he said. Younger ones, he suggested. He and Lizzie were old-timers. It didn't matter what they thought. But through David and Lizzie I saw the very best part of the Amish way of life — the tight family connections and the caring neighbors. The center of their universe was their faith and their children and grandchildren. He loved being Amish, and I believe he felt blessed that his three grown children had joined the church, and that his grandchildren were growing up Amish.

In early September 2007, just as I was wrapping up my trips to the Amish community for this book, he found a lump under his arm and a short time later an oncologist confirmed he had lymphoma again. I and hundreds of others hoped for the very best for his second go-round with cancer, but it scared many of us. Many times I'd drive around his section a time or two to dry my eyes before I pulled into his drive.

The last time I'd talked with him was on the phone. He called from the nearby phone shack to say he had been feeling pretty well and the doctor seemed pleased.

But another call from him a few weeks earlier is one I kept on my cell phone, and at the time I didn't know why. He ended that phone conversation by summing up that the doctor didn't have a lot of encouragement for him to get through the cancer so well this time.

In a very resigned voice he said, "Now it's time to 'prepare to meet thy God.'"

Of course, David did. I'm certain in the days and hours before his death he prepared in earnest for the sudden calling he'd been preaching about for 43 years. So many times in the Amish community, when someone talked about an unexpected death, a tragedy of some kind, they'd address the uncertainty of life with a single phrase "... in the twinkling of an eye ..."

As I stood at the grave site and wept for the loss of a good friend, I thought about that expression. And about the unpredictability of life. I thought of the Amish minister preaching at the funeral, speaking every word in German, but clearly warning—beseeching—the mourners to be prepared. To be mindful that death comes to all. Be ready. It will come in the twinkling of an eye.

I have a hunch that's what David's last sermon, the special one, was about.

And that's why I left the cemetery feeling better about that bright, awesome sky on that terribly sad day. I know he was ready.

I will always remember that picture of David sitting in the yard that evening with his two little granddaughters crawling into his lap, and him saying he had everything in life that he needed. I'll always remember what I learned from him about the hope on the other side. I know for certain David had enough faith in his 67 years, 2 months and 7 days to carry him there.

Acknowledgments

Most of the work on this book was done alongside my regular job as regional editor of The News-Gazette. I couldn't have juggled both without help from News-Gazette staff members Tim Mitchell, Meg Thilmony and Mike Howie, city editor, who covered for me on many shifts.

Meg and Tim also made calls to help get statistics or verify facts, and they listened to countless hours of stories about the Amish experience. I also need to thank Mike Goebel, the copy editor who read over the copy and corrected the misplaced commas and run-on sentences. Darrell Hoemann, photo editor, graciously cleared Vanda Bidwell's schedule so she could make frequent trips to the Arthur-Arcola area. I'm thankful for all the work Amy Eckert did behind-the-scenes with the production and also owe a great thanks to designer Aviva Gold, who brought creativity and a great eye to the project.

Executive Editor John Beck made great suggestions about organizing the book and he also freed me to write most of it. He gave the copy a good careful read, and I value his editing and content suggestions.

The idea for this book originated with Publisher and Editor John Foreman. He initiated the Amish series I wrote for The News-Gazette in 1989, and edited it as well. He decided there was a need to update and expand that project and I'm grateful he asked me to do it. I owe him much, especially for the time he found in his busy schedule to sit and talk during the months this was under way. I appreciate all the crafting and editing suggestions he offered. But mostly, I'm grateful he cared about it nearly as much as I did.

Thanks also to Vanda Bidwell, who pushed herself in some unusual situations to get the photos we needed. She respected the boundaries of the Amish and never crossed the line, and I'm forever grateful for the fine photographs she captured for this book.

My husband Mike helped many times, even counting names and occupations in the Amish directory for me. He made several trips to Arcola and Arthur with me or to pick me up—and never stopped encouraging me. He took over house and horse chores so I could put the time I needed into this project, and never once complained.

Josephine Marner of Chesterville, who grew up in the Amish community but is now Mennonite, helped me track down people and pointed me toward some interesting characters. She also served as my Pennsylvania Dutch interpreter at Amish events, and this book would have been much more challenging without her. I also need to thank longtime friend Phyllis Stock of Arthur, a great resource, who guided and encouraged and helped in the community she's known all her life.

Lastly, I want to thank the Amish people who welcomed me into their homes. I value the time I spent in their kitchens and schools and shops. I had a great time getting to know them and was always treated graciously and warmly. Though the work on this book is finished, I am sure I'll be visiting the community for years to come. I know I'll be shopping there—I've become addicted to Shady Crest's cider and Beachy's whoopie pies—and made special friends, young and not-so-young, that I plan to keep for a lifetime.

A Great Country Bank
in a Great Country

· Two Great ATM Locations

· Drive-Up ATM at Main Bank at 411 South Vine

· Walk-In ATM Gazebo at 114 West Illinois

· Serving the area since 1910

· Arthur's only locally owned and managed bank

We want to be your bank.

State Bank of Arthur

IN A GREAT COUNTRY

ARTHUR, ILLINOIS

411 S. Vine · Arthur, Illinois · 217-543-2111

A GREAT COUNTRY BANK

EQUAL HOUSING LENDER

FDIC

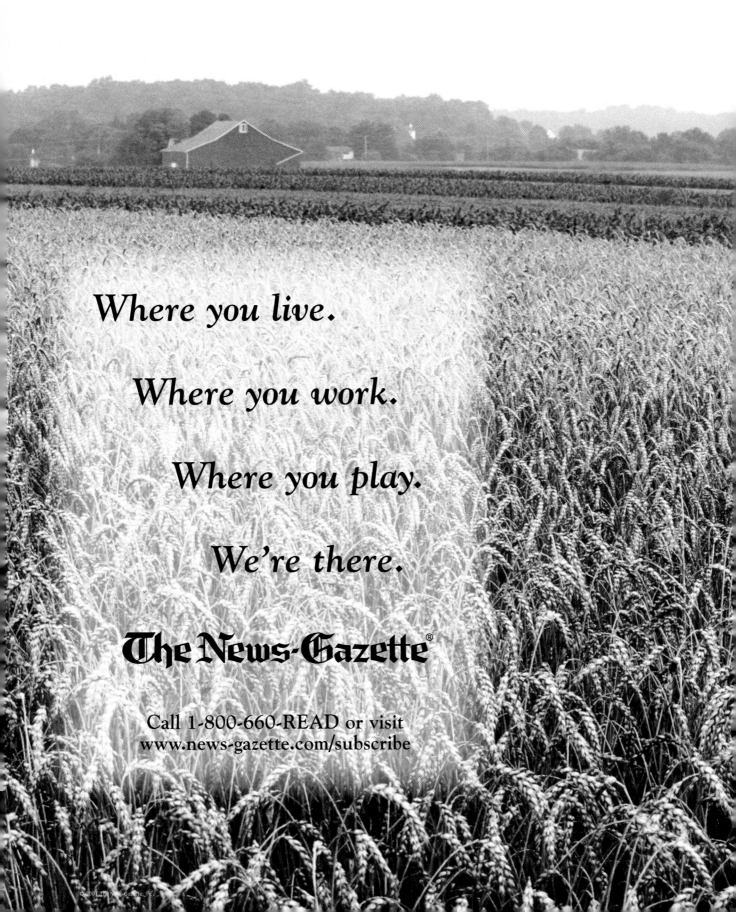